MINIMAL COMPETENCY TESTING

MINIMAL COMPETENCY TESTING

Peter W. Airasian • George F. Madaus • Joseph J. Pedulla

Boston College

**EDUCATIONAL TECHNOLOGY PUBLICATIONS
ENGLEWOOD CLIFFS, NEW JERSEY 07632**

Library of Congress Cataloging in Publication Data

Airasian, Peter W
    Minimal competency testing.

    Includes bibliographies and index.
    1. Competency based educational tests—United
States—Addresses, essays, lectures.   2. Com-
petency based education—United States—
Addresses, essays, lectures.   I. Madaus, George F.,
joint author.   II. Pedulla, Joseph J., joint
author.   III. Title.
LC1034.A36   371.2'64   79-3994
ISBN 0-87778-138-9

Printed in the United States of America.

Library of Congress Catalog Card Number:
79-3994.

International Standard Book Number:
0-87778-138-9.

First Printing: July, 1979.

To

Gwen, Anne, and Barbara

List of Contributors

Peter W. Airasian, Professor, Boston College, School of Education, Chestnut Hill, Massachusetts.

Henry M. Brickell, Director, Policy Studies in Education, Academy for Educational Development, New York, New York.

Walt Haney, The Huron Institute, Cambridge, Massachusetts.

George F. Madaus, Professor, Boston College, School of Education, Chestnut Hill, Massachusetts.

Merle S. McClung, Staff Attorney and Private Education Law Consultant, Center for Law and Education, Cambridge, Massachusetts.

M. Hayes Mizell, Associate Director, Southeastern Public Education Program, American Friends Service Committee, Columbia, South Carolina.

Kenneth B. Newton, Graduate Assistant, Boston College, School of Education, Chestnut Hill, Massachusetts.

Joseph J. Pedulla, Research Associate, Boston College, School of Education, Chestnut Hill, Massachusetts.

Edward F. Reidy, Jr., Director, Project Competency, Fitchburg Public Schools, Fitchburg, Massachusetts.

Preface

The authors of one chapter in this book state, "The minimal competency testing movement is a peculiar phenomenon." And so it is. The movement burst onto the educational scene in the early 1970's and in a few short years has captured the attention not only of educators but of a broad spectrum of the American public as well. It is a movement that is both praised and damned; each passing week sees the debate over its future heighten and sharpen. It is a movement with one overriding goal, that of producing pupils well-grounded in basic skills; but it seeks simultaneously to motivate students, make teachers work harder, increase the cost-effectiveness of education, and instill school accountability. It is a movement that, within its rubric, hides all manner of variation; in some instances, minimal competency means simply early diagnosis and remediation of pupils' learning problems, while in other instances, it means passing a test in order to be promoted from grade to grade, and in still other instances, it means successful performance on an examination as a prerequisite to receipt of a high school diploma. It is a movement which represents the culmination of a diverse set of technical and political events which have transpired in education in the past 15 years and which have raised the level of demand for public accountability and a return to "basics" in American schools. It is a movement in which the rhetoric is predominantly about school and educator culpability but which, in its most prevalent form, applies severest penalties for poor performance to students.

In spite of such anomalies, the minimal competency testing movement holds a certain appeal. The implicit promise of knowledgeable, literate students, well-versed in the "basics," strikes a responsive chord in those segments of the population who look with concern or disfavor on research reports which provide little evidence of school effectiveness, a 14-year decline in Scholastic Aptitude Test scores, educational malpractice suits, and the reality of poorly prepared high school graduates moving into the work force or higher education. When these factors are coupled with the increasing cost of education, declining enrollments, and widespread disaffection for what is perceived by many to be the unstructured, "progressive," and permissive programs pursued in American schools in the last decade, there is little wonder that the vision of competent pupils, well prepared in the basics of reading, writing, and mathematics—not to mention, in some cases, "life skills"—is seductive. Indeed, a further anomaly in the movement is that for the first time in recent memory, the primary impetus for educational change has come from parents and state legislators, rather than from within the educational establishment itself.

In the face of such promises, however, there are numerous questions and potential pitfalls which plague the minimal competency testing movement. At present, the widespread popular support for minimal competency testing resides primarily in the perceived desirability of its ends: cost-effective education; hard-working teachers; and, most of all, pupils able to perform "basic" skills. In this climate, little attention has been focused upon questions related either to the process of education in a competency testing framework or to the potential legal, economic, and moral consequences of such a framework. For example, it seems reasonable to ask, in light of present-day knowledge about instruction and learning, whether schools and teachers possess the ability and techniques necessary to make all or virtually all pupils literate, even in the "basics." More pointedly, is there agreement on what the "basics" are, and if there is not, who should be responsible for determining the topics and skills schools emphasize? Is the measurement technology required to construct competency tests sufficiently developed to permit the use of such tests to make critical decisions about promotion or high school graduation? What exactly is minimal competence and how does one determine it? That is to say, what criteria does one use to distinguish the competent pupil from the incompetent pupil in a fair, reliable, defensible manner? What is a minimal competency testing program likely to cost, both psychically and financially? These and similar questions remain to be answered, but it is evident that their answers will have crucial import for the direction taken by the minimal competency testing movement.

One reason for the uncertainty surrounding minimal competency testing is that although much discussed and debated, it is little practiced, at least on a large scale. Some school districts, Denver, Colorado being the most well-known, have had minimal competency testing programs for over a decade. However, the notion of mandated, state-wide minimal competency testing programs is comparatively recent, and as yet, no state has awarded or denied a pupil a high school diploma on the basis of his or her performance on a competency test. Florida will begin awarding diplomas on the basis of such tests in 1979, California in 1980, and other states soon after. Thus, in some states, minimal competency testing programs are not far from reality, and it appears likely that other states will have some form of program in the near future. As yet, however, because such programs are not yet fully implemented, the resolution of many of the uncertainties associated with minimal competency testing programs must await the perspective gained through experience.

All of this is not to suggest that nothing is known about minimal competency testing programs; in fact, there is a burgeoning literature on the topic. The purpose of this book is to bring together important writings which address the multitude of issues and problems associated with the competency testing movement. The book is intended primarily for local and state educators and school administrators who inevitably will have to confront the movement, as well as for interested lay persons, such as parents and school board members, who have both an interest and a stake in the problems of school standards and pupil learning.

The book is divided into four sections. The first section charts the rise of the minimal competency movement, outlining its goals, history, and politics as well as relating it to recent trends and developments in education. The second section addresses issues and problems associated with the movement. In this section, a series of papers which deal with the conceptual, instructional, curricular, measurement, legal, and cost implications of minimal competency testing programs are presented. Section three provides a comparison of two common models under which competency programs are implemented: a centralized, state administered model, and a local district administered model. A comparison of these models in terms of seven policy issues is provided: (1) state versus local control of education; (2) impact on school curricula; (3) remediation problems; (4) standard setting; (5) measurement issues; (6) legal issues; and (7) costs. The final section of the book provides a summary and recommendations for implementing minimal competency testing programs. We have consciously endeavored to make the contents of each section as pertinent and non-technical as possible so that the book can be used by the wide-ranging and varied audiences for whom the topic of minimal competency testing has import.

We wish to express our gratitude to the Bureau of Research and Assessment of the Massachusetts State Department of Education for allowing us to revise portions of our report, "Policy issues in minimal competency testing and a comparison of implementation models" (April, 1978), dealing with premeasurement concerns, technical issues, costs, and implementation models.

For clerical and secretarial assistance in the production and preparation of the manuscript, we are indebted to Glen Schneiders, whose cheerful and dedicated performance we appreciate greatly.

P.W.A.
G.F.M.
J.J.P.

Table of Contents

Glossary

Accountability—the process in which an individual, group, or institution is held responsible for pupil achievement, usually measured by means of a test.

Affective competencies—behaviors concerned with students' interests, attitudes, values, feelings, dispositions, etc.

Basic skills—traditional school-taught skills in the areas of reading, writing, and mathematics, e.g., add, subtract, multiply, and divide, punctuate and capitalize correctly, etc.

Competencies—statements which identify specific skills, processes, and learnings students are expected to accomplish in school.

Competency-based graduation—a program in which the award of a high school diploma is made contingent upon successful accomplishment of specific, prespecified behaviors.

Concurrent validity—a measure of how well test results correlate with other criteria which might provide the same type of information about test-takers.

Construct validity—the extent to which a test measures one or more dimensions of a trait or theory; an examination of the factors underlying test performance.

Content validity—the extent to which the content of the test items reflects the academic discipline, behavior, or knowledge under study.

Criterion-referenced test—a test on which an individual pupil's performance is interpreted in terms of his or her performance on a set of prespecified objectives or competencies.

Curriculum validity—a measure of the extent to which the test items represent the curriculum to which the test-takers have been exposed.

Cut-off score—that score which serves to differentiate individuals who "pass" and "fail" a test; if the cut-off score is 70, pupils who attain scores below 70 "fail" the test.

Failure rate—the proportion or percentage of students who do not pass a test or examination.

Grade equivalent score—the grade of pupils for which a given score is the average. If a pupil's score on a test is equal to the average score attained by pupils in the sixth month of grade four, his or her grade equivalent score is 4.6.

Instructional validity—a measure of the extent to which the school or school district's stated curriculum objectives were translated into topics actually taught in the school or school district's classrooms.

Life skills—pupil performances which involve the application of school-learned basic skills to real-life situations, e.g., balance a checkbook, write a business letter, complete a job application, etc.

Minimal competency testing—a program in which students are tested to determine their mastery of certain skills defined as essential aspects of school learning or essential for performing tasks routinely confronted in adult life.

Norm-referenced test—a test on which an individual pupil's performance is interpreted in terms of his or her standing relative to the performance of other pupils who took the test.

Phase-in period—the length of time it requires to prepare and install a new program or policy.

Predictive validity—the extent to which predictions made from a test are confirmed by subsequent data or performance.

Reliability—the consistency or accuracy of a test score or a classification made on the basis of a test score.

Remediation—the process in which pupils identified as not having learned certain competencies to a satisfactory level are provided additional instruction or resources to remedy their learning gaps.

School skills—see basic skills.

*Standard score—*a score given in terms of standard deviation units from the mean of a test score distribution; a negative standard score indicates performance below the mean and a positive standard score indicates performance above the mean.

*Standard setting—*the process by which the standard or cut-off score for a minimal competency test is established; standard setting is essentially a judgmental process.

*Standardized test—*a test designed to be administered and scored under uniform conditions; used to obtain comparable measures in different classes or schools and usually interpreted in terms of predetermined norms.

*Standards—*levels of performance; in minimal competency graduation programs, the standard is the lowest score which a student may attain and still be granted a high school diploma; *see* cut-off score.

*State-wide assessment—*a testing program carried out to examine the general level of achievement of pupils in schools throughout the state; usually carried out by sampling schools and pupils for testing.

Survival skills—see life skills.

*Test—*a sample of behavior used to make inferences about a pupil's performance on a larger domain of similar behaviors.

*Validity—*the extent to which a test measures what it is intended to measure; in line with the different purposes of tests, there are different types of validity.

MINIMAL
COMPETENCY
TESTING

Section I: Background

Although the minimal competency testing movement has gained virtual overnight notoriety, its genesis can be traced to a series of movements and events which began in the 1960's. The purposes of the selections in this section are to provide a description of the background of the movement and to introduce a number of general themes which will be explored in greater detail in succeeding sections of the book. The perspective presented in the four following selections helps provide a framework for examining various forms and approaches to minimal competency testing, not only in terms of their actual procedures, but also in terms of the educational problems they are intended to solve.

The first selection, "A Citizen's Introduction to Minimal Competency Testing," poses and answers 23 of the most commonly asked questions about competency testing programs. Starting with a definition of minimal competency testing programs, Mizell takes the reader through the expectations and pitfalls of such programs, the nature of testing as practiced in minimal competency programs (with examples of test items), the consequences associated with failure to pass a competency test, and the possible effects of such tests on pupils, schools, and curricula.

Pedulla and Reidy describe the rise of the minimal competency movement. Their chapter places the initial conceptual impetus for minimal competency testing in the perceptions and events which led to the "back to basics" movement: declining test scores, educational malpractice suits, increased costs for education in the face of declining enrollments, and the unfulfilled promises of innovative educational programs of the 1960's. However, as they point out, from these initial ties to "back to basics," minimal competency testing has attained a life of its own, a life which is quite consistent with wider social emphasis on product standards and quality control.

Airasian explores the technical bases for competency testing. He charts the influence of changing emphases in the areas of educational technology and measurement on the procedures embodied in present competency programs. The rise of the educational objectives and criterion-referenced testing movements are described historically, and their impact on competency testing programs is discussed. The question of setting standards, and the difficulties inherent in establishing cut-off performance scores, are also discussed.

Haney and Madaus provide a broad, critical overview of minimal competency testing in America, focusing upon a variety of general themes and issues underlying the movement. They recount the history and politics of competency testing, its current status, the conceptual and methodological problems of defining, measuring, and certifying pupil competence, and the types of reactions to minimal competency testing which have been forthcoming from various publics and organizations. In conclusion, they seek to provide a glimpse into the future by suggesting new directions and problems for the movement.

These four selections afford a broad and general overview of the minimal competency testing movement which is helpful in placing the remaining sections of this book in proper perspective.

Chapter One

A Citizen's Introduction to
Minimal Competency Testing *

M. Hayes Mizell

1. *What are "minimal competency programs"?*
   "Minimal competency programs" are
   - organized efforts
   - to make sure public school students
   - are able to demonstrate their mastery
   - of certain *minimum* skills
   - needed to perform tasks
   - they will routinely confront in adult life.

2. *What are the components of minimal competency programs?*
   There are many different types of such programs. Though they differ from state to state or from one school district to another, here are some of the features often found in these programs:

*From *A Citizen's Guide to Minimum Competency Testing Programs for Students*. Reprinted with permission of the Southeastern Public Education Program and the author. (For the purpose of stylistic uniformity, the term "Minim*al* Competency Testing" is used throughout this book, instead of "Minim*um* Competency Testing." *Editors' Note*.)

- Statements of the specific skills—such as those needed for reading, writing, and performing mathematical computations—that students are required to master. These are called "performance standards" or "learning objectives." They help pinpoint the competencies schools are responsible for teaching *all* children.
- Tests to determine if students have mastered the required skills; or tests to diagnose the specific skills in which the students may be weak. The term "minimal competency testing" is often used.
- Requirements that students cannot advance to the next grade, cannot graduate from school, or cannot receive a regular diploma if they cannot demonstrate their mastery of the required minimal skills.
- Requirements that students must take a special remedial course if they cannot demonstrate their mastery of the skills.

3. *Why am I reading and hearing so much about the need for minimal competency programs in public schools?*

Pressures to find ways to assure that high school graduates have mastered certain basic, minimum skills come from several quarters:

- Many *parents* are disturbed when they find their children cannot read, write, or compute at a level the parents think is necessary.
- Many *educators* are concerned because high school students' scores on standardized tests, such as the Scholastic Aptitude Test, are declining.
- Many *college instructors* are upset when they find some students can't write a coherent paragraph.
- Many *employers* are angry when young job applicants can't fill out an application, follow simple written directions, or can't read well enough to perform even simple job tasks.

These collective experiences have created a concern that too many students graduating from public schools do not have or cannot apply the basic skills needed to function effectively in our society.

4. *What is meant by "some high school students do not have or cannot apply the skills needed to function in society"?*

There are certain tasks that are fundamental to functioning as an adult member of society. These can include:

- being responsible for routine, personal, homemaking, and business affairs;
- communicating with others;
- pursuing secondary education (formal or self-directed);
- getting and holding a job; and
- fulfilling the duties of responsible citizenship.

In order to perform these tasks, specific skills are necessary. An adult must be able to read well enough to scan the "want-ads" in a newspaper and follow instructions to get and hold a job. He or she must be able to write well enough to fill out a job application, or write a letter.

And he or she must be able to do mathematics well enough to pay bills, to know how much money has been spent or is on hand, and to perform simple household calculations. *Reading, writing, and calculating well enough to perform these basic tasks is what is meant by having minimal competencies.* Using these skills in daily adult life is what is meant by applying the skills in order to function in society.

5. *Who decides what skills and tasks are minimally necessary?*

In states and local school districts which have adopted minimal competency programs, these decisions have been made by either a state legislature, a state board of education, a division of a state department of education, or by a local school board. Because each of these groups is a public body accountable in some way to citizens, there is an opportunity for citizens to have a voice in determining the content of minimal competency programs.

6. *If there are students who have not mastered or who cannot apply basic skills, what can be done?*

There are many options, not all of which are desirable. Schools have responded and are responding to this problem in a variety of ways. They might:

- encourage or allow students who have not mastered or who cannot apply basic skills to drop out of school;
- not allow students to graduate until they can demonstrate their mastery and use of basic skills;
- not allow students to receive a regular high school diploma;
- not allow students to be promoted from one grade level to the next;
- do nothing; allow students to be promoted or graduated without having mastered basic skills or without having demonstrated they can apply them; or
- assign such students to a less demanding curriculum or "track."

Each of the above responses penalizes the students involved, but does not assure the students will ultimately master basic skills as a result of the penalty.

Other schools might choose to:

- identify students' weaknesses in specific basic skill areas early in the students' school career, and continuously throughout, and provide them with special assistance to develop the required skills;
- provide students with individualized instruction utilizing one or more of the following: teachers' aides, programmed instruction, peer instruction, significantly smaller classes, special materials, skill labs, etc.;
- require such students to attend summer school;
- establish tutoring programs to provide such students with special help after school; .
- work with parents to teach them how to help their children learn basic skills at home; or
- assign such students to special classes which devote more time and effort to emphasizing the mastery and use of basic skills in working with the regular course content.

The above efforts may or may not cause students to be able to master and apply basic skills, but at least the focus is on providing help to the students.

Minimal competency programs sometimes involve one or more of the responses listed in both of the above groups.

7. What do people hope minimal competency programs will achieve?

There are several attitudes and motives held by those supporting minimal competency programs. These include the following:

Minimal competency programs will help those children who have the greatest educational needs. It is argued that the educational needs of many underachieving students have often been ignored or inappropriately met by school systems. Minimal competency programs are seen as a way to require school systems to identify who these students are and to focus more attention, energy, and resources on properly responding to their basic educational needs. Many parents of minority and disadvantaged students hold this view because they feel the schools have not given their children enough attention and have allowed them to "slide by" without mastering essential basic skills.

Minimal competency programs will motivate students and stop "social promotions." Some people believe too many students put forth too little effort in school because they know they will be promoted or graduated regardless of how well they perform. When this happens, it is called "social promotion." As a result, some students do not acquire the basic skills they need. It is hoped that if all students are required to demonstrate their mastery of certain minimal competencies before they can be promoted or graduated, this will put an end to "social promotion." It is also hoped these requirements will motivate students to work harder to learn the skills necessary to pass competency tests.

Minimal competency programs will define more precisely what skills must be taught and learned. Holding school systems accountable has been difficult because it often has not been clear specifically what teachers are expected to teach or what students are expected to learn. Minimal competency programs can establish certain learning objectives at the state level or require local school districts to develop them for specific subject areas. Students will then know what they must learn. Parents will have benchmarks against which to measure their children's progress. And teachers can focus more attention on teaching those specific skills.

Minimal competency programs will certify that students have specific minimal competencies. Employers used to rely on high school diplomas to certify that students could read, write, and compute at acceptable levels of competence. Now, however, many employers have complained that even high school graduates do not always have basic competencies necessary in business and industry. Minimal competency programs tied to graduation requirements may restore confidence that a diploma means competency in certain areas. Where not tied to graduation requirements, minimal competency programs may at least aid employers who want to identify those students who do and do not have certain minimal skills.

8. *What are the arguments against minimal competency programs?*
There are many concerns about minimal competency programs. Among those heard most frequently are the following:

Minimal competency programs will exclude more children from schools and further stigmatize and harm underachieving youth. Minimal competency programs can be punitive and exclusionary if they are used simply to deny students promotion or graduation. There is a concern that students who perform poorly on the competency tests will not receive the kind of help they need, and they will be branded as failures and drop out of school. This is especially worrisome for students who do not perform well on paper-and-pencil tests, which is the format of most minimal competency tests. Another concern is that minimal competency programs will be used to certify a student's *lack* of prescribed competencies, which may result in many academically marginal youth becoming unemployable. Children who have historically been shortchanged by the schools—minorities, the low-income, and the disadvantaged—are particularly vulnerable to these abuses.

Minimal competency programs will not assure that children will receive effective remediation. Identifying students' academic problems is only the first step in providing them the help they need. Money, training, and personnel are then necessary to provide students with special help to strengthen their skills. There is no guarantee adequate resources will be provided for such efforts through minimal competency programs. Even if such resources are available, educators have had great difficulty in establishing effective remedial programs. Few effective remedial programs have been developed and maintained by most school systems.

Minimal competency programs oversimplify the competency issue. Questions have been raised about the wisdom of placing so much emphasis on the "basics" when there are so many other factors essential to a successful adjustment to adult life and work. The educational process is exceedingly complex, and it is naive to believe that "essential" competencies can be isolated and tested.

Minimal competency programs will result in curricula becoming too narrow. Similarly, there is concern that so much emphasis on basic skills will narrow school curricula. This means less attention will be devoted to providing a broad range of important educational experiences for young people. Youngsters who perform poorly in academic subjects, but who may excel in other subject areas in which they are more talented, may suffer the most.

Minimal competency programs will place the burden for "failure" on students. Under the provisions of many minimal competency programs, it is the students who must bear the heaviest burden for their unsatisfactory performance on a competency test. This is seen as another example of "blaming the victim" because even though it may be schools which have failed to meet the students' basic skill needs, it is students who are denied promotion or graduation, or who are unfairly labeled. Legislators, school board members, administrators, or teachers are not subject to comparable penalties for their failure to create necessary programs, provide quality instruction, or appropriate the money that will help students learn the basic skills. Thus, if students do not master the competencies expected of them, they are the ones who receive the blame and punishment, while others who may be at least partially responsible for poor student performance are not held accountable.

Minimal competency programs will cause educators to be held unfairly accountable. Another perspective is that of school officials and classroom teachers who believe they may be evaluated and held accountable on the basis of how their students perform on a minimal competency test. A test score alone, however, would not take into account other factors affecting students' competencies. Such factors may include the curriculum, school resources, the students' family background and home environment, etc. Classroom teachers point out that they have no control over these factors.

Minimal competency programs will encourage teachers to "teach the test." Teachers may be under so much pressure to have their students score well on minimal competency tests that they may spend most of their time teaching the students the very limited and specific skills needed to do well on the tests. The effect of this may be that students can successfully complete competency tests but still may not be able to apply those skills to other situations, or learn the range of skills they need.

Minimal competency programs will cause the "minimum" to become the "maximum." The use of minimal competency programs may result in a curriculum which will no longer challenge students who are capable of exceeding the "minimum." There are concerns that schools are already doing too little to challenge such students. The initiation of minimal competency programs may signal to average and above average students that the schools have lowered their expectations of them. As a result, these students may no longer work as hard because they will know they can "get by" so long as they demonstrate their mastery of the minimal competencies required. This may cause the additional problem that students who can meet these minimal requirements may want to graduate from school early because, they may argue, they have met the basic requirements set by the schools. Thus, the question of how high or low to set the "minimum" is an important issue.

9. What do minimal competency tests try to measure?

Minimal competency tests can measure "school skills" and/or

how school skills are applied to real-life situations ("life tasks"):

"School skills." In these tests, students are asked to respond to test items which call for a straightforward use of skills learned in school. They probably do not test the student's ability to apply the skills learned in school to a life situation. Thus, a test for "school skills" may determine that a student knows how to add and subtract, but that does not necessarily mean the student can balance a checkbook. These test items may not be too different from those found on typical school achievement tests except that they are designed only to test the student's *minimum* competencies.   or

"Life tasks" (or, *"life skills"*). In these tests, the students are asked to respond to questions which simulate situations they may encounter in adult life. For example, they may be asked to complete a part of an application for a job or to check the addition on a grocery bill.

10. *Do minimal competency tests measure anything other than students' competencies in reading, writing, and math?*

It depends on what your state legislature, your state board of education, or your local school board determines are the important competencies students should have. Citizens' opinions of what are the essential competencies may differ from those of the representative bodies listed above.

Most people agree it is important for students to be competent in: reading, writing, and mathematics/computation.

However, in some places people believe it is also important for students to be able to demonstrate their competencies in: Health, Citizenship, Personal and Family Finances, Civic and Social Responsibility, Listening, Oral Expression, Family Life, Analyzing, Environmental Protection, Energy Conservation, and Human Relations.

11. *When would students be tested in a minimal competency program?*

It differs from place to place, and this is another area where citizen input is valuable in shaping the program.

Currently, in some school districts, the students must take and pass a test in the twelfth grade in order to qualify for graduation or a regular diploma. Testing so late in the students' school career gives additional information to students, parents, and employers about students' actual performance levels. However, it doesn't allow for any remedial work to help the students make up their learning gaps, or help the school change its curriculum or the teaching styles of its teachers.

Minimal competency programs are more likely to be helpful to students in those districts where tests are administered periodically during the students' school career. In some states, students are tested in grades 1, 3, 6, 9, and 11. Other states test less frequently, such as in grades 4 and 8.

12. *Can you give examples of what might be included on a minimal competency test?*

Yes. Some tasks ask for a direct application of "school skills." The following are sample questions from the "Proficiency and Review" test in Denver, Colorado:

1. Add the following sets of numbers:

   978   The correct answer is:
   669
   435   (A) 2568   (B) 2569   (C) 2659
   + 587
   ─────   (D) 2669   (E) NONE

2. If you think a word is misspelled, circle the letter before it. If you think all the words are spelled correctly, circle the letter before NONE:

   (A) touch   (B) message   (C) choclate

   (D) yourself   (E) NONE

3. This question measures ability to recognize correct English. There are three types of errors: punctuation, capitalization, and grammar. Each line in the following passage is numbered and represents one test question. Mark each line according to

the following key: P for an error in punctuation, C for an error in capitalization, G for an error in grammar, and N for no error.

(A) Have you ever went to a flea

(B) market. Sandmore High School will have the

(C) second International Flea Market on Saturday.

13. *Are all competency tests like that?*

No. Other tests ask students to apply school skills to real-life tasks, such as these sample questions from a test developed by the Educational Testing Service:

1. A job pays $6.50 per hour with time-and-a-half for overtime. If you work 40 regular hours and eight overtime hours at that job, how much would you earn?

   (A) $360 (B) $312 (C) $338 (D) $468

2. An advertisement: Pine Grove Camp Needs Counselors
   Please apply in writing to:
   Morgan Davis
   10 Lincoln Road
   Louisville, Kentucky 40202

   Directions: Thomas Moore is 17. He lives at 69 Banberry Lane in Louisville, Kentucky 40202. He has worked as a counselor at Camp Pioneer for two years. He has been trained in first-aid and water safety.

   Pretend that you are Thomas Moore and write a letter applying for the job of counselor at Pine Grove Camp.

3. A warning on a medicine label may read:

   Severe sore throat or sore throat accompanied by fever, headache, nausea, or vomiting may be serious. Consult a physician immediately. If rash or irritation develops, stop using and consult a physician. Do not use more than five days or give to children under three years of age unless directed by a physician.

According to the label, if you have a sore throat, fever, and a headache, you should:

(A) use the medicine for five days.
(B) call a doctor as soon as you can.
(C) increase the amount of medicine you take.
(D) use other medication to cure the fever and headache.

14. *Aren't most schools giving minimal competency tests now?*

Not exactly. At present, most tests given in schools are either developed (1) by individual classroom teachers, or (2) by national test publishers.

The tests developed by individual classroom teachers usually test only those skills or facts which the teacher thinks the students should be able to demonstrate based on what the teacher has taught in his or her classroom. These are called "criterion-referenced" tests. One problem in using them as minimal competency tests is that they vary widely from one classroom to another. One sixth grade teacher of math may expect more of his or her students, and design a test accordingly, than another math teacher in the same school teaching students of the same grade level. Not only do the "minimums" which are tested vary from one teacher to another, but the quality of the tests differ as well.

Tests developed by national publishers (such as the popular achievement tests, for example, the Comprehensive Test of Basic Skills or the Iowa Test of Basic Skills) are designed to test many different levels of students' performance, not just minimum. But, more importantly, they are what are known as "norm-referenced" tests, and only tell how well a student performed compared to other students. They give no useful information on whether a student can perform a particular skill. If the students on whom the test was "normed" all had low skill levels in reading, for example, it would be possible for a student to have a relatively high score and still not read well enough to function in adult life.

15. *If a student passes the minimal competency test required for graduation from high school, does this mean the student is able to perform at the twelfth grade level?*

No. Most minimal competency requirements for graduation are designed only to assure that the student can successfully complete the specific items included on the test. These represent the *minimal* level of performance acceptable, not what high school graduates should have learned in other areas or even what the average twelfth grader knows. Most of the people who construct these tests believe that the items represent skills necessary for adult literacy. (This usually corresponds to what students are expected to know when they are in the seventh or eighth grade.)

Note that because the tests measure *minimal* levels of skills, they don't tell you how well some students can do, nor the range of skills from "minimally acceptable" to "best." Students who have passed them and have received a regular high school diploma will perform at many different levels. One student may be able to perform at a level expected of an eighth grader, while another may be able to function at a level expected of a junior in college.

16. *What happens if a student doesn't "pass" the competency test?*

Again, this depends on the provisions of a particular state or school district. Citizen input is critical in determining this aspect of minimal competency programs.

In some places, if the student does not perform satisfactorily on the competency test, he or she simply doesn't receive a regular diploma. (He or she may receive a special certificate of attendance.)

In other places, the student may receive remedial help, or may have to take a special course. Many minimal competency programs allow the student to take the test again after receiving remedial help.

Some state minimal competency laws address this problem. Colorado law requires schools to provide extra tutorial assistance to students. California law requires students to be provided with remedial assistance and for parent-teacher-principal-student conferences to be held to discuss the problem.

17. *How effective are remedial programs?*

The problem with such programs is that many school districts lack well-developed remedial programs in the basic skills—especially at the secondary school level.

It is one thing to require that students who fail the competency test receive remedial help, but it is quite another matter to develop an *effective* remedial program. The problem is underscored when one considers that many of the students who are most likely to fail a minimal competency test are those who have been receiving some form of remedial help anyway. The challenge clearly will be how to use the information the tests will provide in a constructive manner, and how to improve and support the special programs some students will need.

18. *If minimal competency programs require that local school districts provide special programs for those who do not pass the tests, who will pay for such programs?*

This is unclear. The state legislature would have to provide funds for such programs or local school districts would have to find or raise money to finance them. In the past, local school districts have complained when state legislatures passed laws requiring the districts to initiate new educational programs but provided no new state monies to help pay for those programs. The lack of money could become an excuse for inaction on the part of the districts. Of course, the intended benefits of any minimal competency program would be seriously undermined if there were a requirement that students not passing the test should receive remedial help only to find districts were giving "lip service" to this requirement in the absence of any state funds to finance such programs.

However, there are those who feel that few additional resources are necessary and that schools could accomplish a great deal by simply redirecting monies that are now used in ineffective attempts to teach students. Such instructional strategies as "peer teaching" (more skilled students helping teach less skilled students on an individual basis) might be used in the absence of more money.

19. *Can you explain more about how minimal competency programs are related to concerns about "social promotion"?*

Many citizens perceive "social promotion" as a cause of public school graduates not having skills the public thinks are essential. "Social promotion" refers to the practice of allowing students to advance to the next grade even if they have not mastered the academic skills taught in the lower grade. The promotion, in other words, tends to be based more on the student's age than on what he or she has demonstrated he or she has learned.

In the past, this practice has been defended on the basis that it was not realistic to retain students in the same grade year after year. Such retentions often resulted in over-age students being in the same classroom with much younger children. It has been the opinion of many educators that such retained students do not have the opportunity for healthy social and emotional development, and that they suffer from the stigma of having to remain back a grade while their classmates go on to the next grade. The effect of such a stigma has been that often these students are branded as failures, develop a poor self-concept, and drop out of school.

During the 1975-76 school year in one Southern state, half of the students who dropped out of school had also repeated one or more grades. Thus, many educators contend that "retaining" a student does not solve the student's motivational or learning problems.

20. *Well, is "social promotion" good or bad?*

Think of it in terms of what the child really needs. "Social promotion" is not good if it becomes a cop-out for the school with the result that the child's real academic and emotional needs are ignored. Obviously, it does the child no good if he or she is passed along through the school system without ever having his or her real needs diagnosed and met, and that has too often been the case.

On the other hand, there is certainly no guarantee that the child's needs *will* be met just because he or she is "retained" at a particular grade level. If the school and its personnel have no commitment, plan, or resources for dealing with the child the second year he or she is in a grade that significantly differs from the way he or she was dealt with the first year he or she was in that same grade, then holding the child back will not likely help.

Meeting children's needs is not so simple as either promoting them or failing them. "Retaining" a student is usually meant to frighten, punish, or motivate the child, but it does not necessarily require the school or its personnel to do anything different to assure that the child will get the help he or she needs. Thus, the real emphasis should be on creating and supporting a system which requires schools more intensively to diagnose and address the needs of children who do not meet the minimal competency requirements.

If children are really to be helped and to be able to perform minimal competencies, then the schools must have the commitment and capacity to give special attention to those children, regardless of whether they are promoted or "retained." Many children are not now receiving such attention. Of course, providing special attention requires strong and dedicated school administrators, good teachers, and money. A minimal competency program may help to better focus the resources which are presently available, but it is no substitute for more committed and skilled educators or for the money which is needed to train and employ such professionals.

21. *Are there other reasons people are now so interested in minimal competency programs?*

Yes. Some believe the value of a high school diploma has been "cheapened" because even students with a diploma cannot necessarily read, write, or compute well enough to succeed in a job. It is the opinion of many such people that only students who have clearly demonstrated their mastery of basic skills should receive a high school diploma. Other students who have attended public school for 12 years but have not mastered the basic skills should receive some kind of certificate of attendance, it is argued.

22. *Are the concerns about the value of a high school diploma valid?*

It depends on what is considered to be the purpose of a high school diploma. Some people, especially employers of high school graduates, want the diploma to be a convenient screening device or a guarantee which assures them the job applicant has certain basic skills. In other words, they want the diploma to be a *certificate* which, in effect, says the job applicant can perform certain basic skills. But, in reality, a diploma is a piece of paper which reveals very little about an individual's competency.

Some educators contend that it is wrong to think of the diploma as a document which certifies that the bearer has certain competencies. They say the diploma is really nothing more than an award for the student completing the course requirements the state has mandated. If you want to know whether a person is competent, these educators say, and what competencies the individual has, then it is necessary to examine the transcript of that person, as well as look at his or her record of performance in extra-curricular activities and talk with some of the educators who have taught and worked with that person.

Most of us would like to think there is a simple way of sorting out the potentially good workers from the bad ones, and the most competent from the least competent, but it is probably too much to expect that a high school diploma alone can provide the convenient means for making such determinations.

As members of the general public, we all know doctors, lawyers, teachers, barbers, and scholars who have diplomas hanging on their walls, but we have all had experiences which would cause us to doubt that these diplomas mean all such individuals are competent.

23. *What effect will minimal competency programs have on a school's curriculum?*

It seems logical that if students are to be tested to determine their mastery of certain skills, then the curricula of individual schools will have to reflect the new emphasis on those skills. Adjustments in what is taught, how it is taught, and the amount of time teaching it may be necessary. This will particularly be the case in those schools where significant numbers of students do not meet the minimal competency requirements. However, if a school implements the competency program in a way that places the burden of failure and the need for remediation only on the shoulders of those students who perform poorly, then few changes in the curriculum may occur.

Chapter Two

The Rise of the Minimal
Competency Testing Movement

Joseph J. Pedulla*
Edward F. Reidy, Jr.

To many parents, businessmen, and citizens, as well as to most educators and legislators across the country, "competency testing" has become a "household word." With unprecedented speed and with no identifiable leaders in the field of education, the competency testing movement has captured the enthusiastic endorsement of citizens, politicians, and educational policy-makers in the majority of the 50 states. This movement, led not by educators, but by citizens and their political representatives, is one aspect of a larger "back to basics" movement that is prevalent throughout the country. How did the competency movement come to be and to obtain such a strong hold on present-day educational planning and practice? In this chapter, we trace the rise of the competency testing movement.

We feel that much of the impetus behind the minimal competency movement stems from perceptions of various publics that standards in public schools are falling. This chapter outlines the perceptions that have given rise to the demand for a return to

*The order of the authors is strictly alphabetical.

23

basics and for minimal competency testing. We shall not discuss the validity of these perceptions, and in many cases we feel that the "facts" do not necessarily support people's beliefs about the quality of schools. However, whether the perceptions are correct or not, that they are widely held makes them a special type of "fact." They describe a structure of values and attitudes which is every bit as real as the condition of school buildings, number of teachers, test score distributions, etc. Even more important is that these perceptions are the ultimate determiners of what happens. Programs evolve in the context of the value-based perceptions of people. To put the point more directly, when people perceive the facts as real, they are real in their consequences; perceptions widely held can become "facts" and causes of action. The opinions and perceptions of people about the current status of our schools has, we feel, given rise to an action program, the minimal competency testing movement.

Back to Basics

The past five years have seen a steady rise in the public's dissatisfaction with public education. There are many reasons for this dissatisfaction, and one must understand these reasons to understand why the competency testing movement has gained tremendous grass-roots support.

One source of this growing dissatisfaction was the news of declining test scores, in particular, tests used for college admissions. Reports of score declines have appeared in the media and been interpreted as evidence that the quality of schooling has deteriorated (Armbruster, 1977; Harnischfeger and Wiley, 1975; Wirtz, 1977). Whether test scores of this type represent an adequate basis for making judgments about the quality of schooling is a separate issue (cf. Madaus, Airasian, and Kellaghan, in press). The fact remains that a large percentage of the American public *believes* that such score declines are indicative of a decline in the quality of education.

During the period of the test score decline, the percentage of A and B grades awarded students has consistently and dramatically increased, while the percentage of failing grades has decreased.

This grade inflation has contributed to the public's perception that standards in education have deteriorated (Brodinsky, 1977; Neill, 1978).

Against this backdrop of a growing belief that standards are falling, the cost of public education has become a major focal point of community dissatisfaction. Since 1960, the cost of public schooling has soared (Neill, 1978), exceeding the consumer price index. The burden of these increased costs has been borne largely by local property owners. Confronted by highly visible, ever-increasing costs, at a time of declining school enrollment, taxpayers have begun to ask for evidence of concomitant increases in the quality of schooling. During a period of high inflation, the double barreled issues of runaway school costs and a decline in the number of students assumed increased importance in countless communities. The perception grew that taxpayers were paying more and getting less, particularly in terms of the basic skills achievement of their children.

Further, at a time of recession, high inflation, and high unemployment, a crescendo of employer complaints began to be heard about the inability of many high school graduates to read, write, and compute. College teachers complained that students entering college lacked basic cognitive skills. Colleges found it necessary to increase dramatically the number of remedial courses. Finally, it was found that 13 percent of adult Americans were functionally illiterate (Neill, 1978; Southeastern Public Education Program, 1978). It is no wonder that the cry that education should return to basics was heard throughout the land.

. During the same period, students and their parents began to bring lawsuits against school districts on the grounds that they or their offspring received a high school diploma, yet had trouble reading and writing (Neill, 1978). Although these educational malpractice suits were few in number and none of the court rulings to date have been in favor of the plaintiffs, they received widespread publicity which further eroded the public's confidence in the schools. The very fact that suits were brought in the first place fed public sentiment that schools were not doing an adequate job teaching basic skills. Moreover, the threat of additional suits prompted school administrators to examine their curricula and to increase their focus on the basic skills.

To many Americans, it was clear that the educational promises of the sixties were unfulfilled. The public's belief in the power of education as a mechanism for personal and social reform had been raised to an unrealistic, unattainable level. The billions of federal dollars poured into programs for compensatory education, drop-out prevention, nutrition, and various "innovative" approaches to teaching had not produced the dramatic impact promised by the reformers of the sixties (Averch, Carroll, Donaldson, Kiesling, and Pincus, 1974). Many felt that the schools had spread themselves too thin by endeavoring to provide services which formerly belonged to the family, the church, and community and social agencies. Instead of concentrating on their primary task of teaching basic skills, schools were perceived by many as being involved in too many peripheral areas.

Since the turn of the century, a primary policy focus of American education has been to increase the proportion of pupils who complete 12 grades of education and receive a high school diploma. We have been reasonably successful in attaining this goal: in 1900, fewer than ten percent of the 17-year-olds completed high school; in 1940, roughly half of the 17-year-olds completed high school; and by 1965, about 75 percent of the 17-year-olds completed high school, a level that has remained quite constant to the present day (Green, 1977). However, this dramatic increase in the proportion of pupils graduating from high school has not been without costs. Over the years, in order to accommodate pupils of increasing heterogeneity, the requirement for high school gradua-tion has shifted largely to one of attendance; students who were present in school for the necessary number of days and who had accumulated sufficient credits were virtually guaranteed a high school diploma. Social promotion has been the rule and, particu-larly in the past 15 years, the quality of the courses students took and the standards for acceptable performance in these courses are perceived by many people to have declined dramatically. More-over, the proliferation of courses at the secondary level allowed many students to amass the required number of credits for graduation while avoiding more rigorous courses involving reading, writing, and mathematics.

Public dissatisfaction is widespread in regard to social promotion, graduation based on attendance rather than achievement, and curricula which are perceived to be watered down. This dissatisfaction, compounded by declining test scores, grade inflation, employer complaints about the skills of high school graduates, college teachers' concern with the level of training of entering students, the soaring costs of public education in conjunction with declining enrollment, the unfulfilled promises of compensatory and innovative educational programs, and educational malpractice suits have combined to produce demands that the schools concentrate more on teaching the basic skills and further that they provide *proof* that students are learning these skills.

It should be noted again that many of the issues just cited are *perceived* as problems by many people. It may well be that some are not, in fact, real problems or that information or data have been misinterpreted. Nevertheless, it is undeniable that public dissatisfaction with schools stems from such perceptions. The fact that many people perceive basic skills as needing more emphasis has been enough by itself to make schools increase their concentration on basics and to impel state legislators to enact minimal competency testing legislation.

The call is for abandoning social promotion and attendance as the principal criteria for awarding a diploma. As Thomas Green (1977) has pointed out,

> If we cannot discriminate between people on the basis of the *level* of the system that they attain, nonetheless we can discriminate between them on the basis of *how* that level was reached. In other words, we have reached a point in the development of education in which we discover that it is not the *level* of the system that matters, but the *quality* of the education pursued in reaching this level (p. 8).

Concentrating efforts upon having high proportions of pupils complete high school has lessened concern over standards and the meaning and value of the diploma (Green, 1977).

In the past, the response of school administrators to such criticisms was that they were merely doing what the public wanted them to do; but the mood of the public has changed. Emphasis on the basic skills is apparently what a large segment of the public wants. Most citizens believe that the schools can do a good job of teaching reading, writing, and arithmetic if they would concentrate more on that job.

Public demands that teachers teach and pupils learn the basics have been met in many ways. In some schools, increased time and emphasis have been devoted to instruction in reading, writing, and arithmetic; in others, efforts are underway to make the teacher's role more dominant and to increase structure and discipline in the classroom. There is a revival of older methods of instruction; an emphasis on drill, recitation, homework, and frequent testing. Some schools have limited or eliminated social promotion and have begun to promote pupils primarily on the basis of their achievement in basic cognitive skills. Still other schools have begun to eliminate "frills" from their curricula, while others have reduced the time spent on "social services," such as sex and drug education, and used the time for increased instruction in reading, writing, and arithmetic. All of these approaches and others have been adopted in an effort to accede to the public's request that the schools place greater emphasis on the basics.

Minimal Competency Testing

The demand that schools provide proof that students are learning the basics has been met with an increased emphasis on testing, particularly minimal competency testing. The emphasis accorded testing may seem strange in light of the fact that testing is under attack by many educators and educational groups. Yet, a recent Gallup poll showed an overwhelming majority of the public in favor of requiring students to pass a test as a prerequisite to receiving a high school diploma (Gallup, 1977).

Perhaps if the "back to basics" movement had had its roots within the educational community, there would be considerably less emphasis upon minimal competency *testing*. But as we begin to understand the reasons why the "back to basics" movement has emerged, we also begin to see clearly that the impetus for change has come from groups outside of the educational community. For these groups, it would not be enough to request only that schools spend more time on the basics. In the face of widespread disillusionment with the public schools, there is a need, indeed a demand, for *external* assurances that the basics are being mastered. Since the perceived deterioration in standards and pupil performance has been based to a large extent on test score declines, it was only reasonable to many people that the success of schools in promoting the basics be documented in terms of test performance also.

Moreover, for many people, test results are a common yardstick used to measure school success; tests and schooling seem to go hand in hand. Everyone who has attended school has taken many tests. Yet minimal competency tests represent a different breed of test from the teacher-made or standardized tests familiar to most people. Teacher-made tests are designed for use with the teacher's own class, either to assign grades to students or to determine where more instructional emphasis is needed. Standardized tests usually are administered system-wide to place students, to identify very high or very low achievers, or to obtain an indication of the average achievement of students at a particular grade level across the school district. Minimal competency tests, on the other hand, are intended primarily to make a decision about each student's attainment of some desired level of competence.

One of the features which makes minimal competency testing attractive is the presumption that it can certify that the individual student meets certain performance standards. The tests are seen as useful means of providing proof that a student can read, write, or compute; through use of such tests, the diploma can, in business parlance, become a type of product warranty.

Concern over proof of quality and standards has gained importance in non-educational areas, as witnessed by various consumer protection laws and mandated product safety standards. One finds examples of standards of adequacy in the area of food additives. Additives are *tested* for potentially harmful effects to humans and if found to be harmful must either be eliminated from all foods sold in the United States or must be present in prescribed limits, i.e., *standards* of safety are set. Countless other examples of this scenario can be cited for various products (e.g., toys, automobiles, power tools), foods, drugs, and the environment. In all instances, *tests* are conducted, products are certified as adequate or inadequate, and some action is taken on the basis of this certification. When recent concern over the quality of student learning arose, we should not have been surprised when the public asked for the same type of evidence or proof of quality that it had come to expect of consumer products.

In light of this expectation, the existing precedent for testing in schools, and the perceived need for more emphasis on basic skills, should we have expected anything other than a minimal competency test as a certification mechanism? If there is a question as to whether students have acquired the skills and knowledge which the public or community deem important for grade-to-grade promotion or high school graduation, then the sentiment is that students should be tested to determine which ones do not have these skills so that some form of corrective action may be taken. Minimal competency tests are perceived by many to be an ideal prescription for this problem. Given that we can test food additives and identify where corrective action is necessary, there is a belief that we ought to be able to carry out the same procedure with students.

Interestingly, minimal competency testing programs have had spin-offs into non-basic skill areas. The whole educational process is being re-examined, and some groups have identified areas, such as citizenship and so-called "survival skills" (e.g., balancing a checkbook, completing a tax form or job application, planning nutritious meals, etc.), as desired competencies for high school graduates. Thus, the calls for more emphasis on basics and for testing these basics have in turn led to testing areas beyond those normally considered to involve basic skills. Although this sequence of events appears anomalous, it is a fact, and it results from different groups using the competency movement to promote their own interests.

In summary, dissatisfaction with the perceived quality of education has resulted in a critical examination of the educational process by the general public. This examination has led to the perception, rightly or wrongly, that basic skills instruction is deficient. This perception in turn has resulted in demands that more emphasis be placed on the basics and that schools provide proof that students are learning the basics to adequate levels of mastery. Many people, conditioned by their own educational experiences with tests as well as by non-educational experiences, think about quality in terms of tests and standards and this is a primary thrust behind the competency testing movement. Although the transfer from testing product or food quality to testing educational quality seems straightforward, it is not. Since it is people who are being tested, and not tires, cans of food, or additives, a whole series of problems that do not arise in product testing becomes important. Similarly, the transfer from school tests with which most adults are familiar to minimal competency tests is not straightforward and results in problems that must be addressed. Later sections of this book present discussions of these problems as they pertain to the issue of minimal competency testing as a means of providing proof that schools are successfully teaching desired skills to students. It seems clear that the minimal competency testing movement is with us and is likely to remain with us for many years. The genesis of the minimal competency testing movement as it has emerged from the "back to basics" movement is fairly straightforward. What is less straightforward, however, is whether the minimal competency testing movement can and will attain the promise so many citizens hold for it.

References

Armbruster, F.E. *Our children's crippled future.* N.Y.: Quadrangle/The New York Times Book Co., 1977.

Averch, H.A., Carroll, S.J., Donaldson, T.S., Kiesling, H.J., & Pincus, J. *How effective is schooling? A critical review of research.* Englewood Cliffs, N.J.: Educational Technology Publications, 1974.

Brodinsky, B. Back to basics: The movement and its meaning. *Phi Delta Kappan,* March, 1977, 522-527.

Gallup, G.H. Ninth annual Gallup poll of the public's attitudes

toward the public schools. *Phi Delta Kappan,* September, 1977,
33-48.

Green, T.F. Minimal educational standards: A systemic perspective. Paper for four regional conferences sponsored by the
Education Commission of the States and the National Institute
of Education, Fall, 1977.

Harnischfeger, A., & Wiley, D.E. *Achievement test score decline:
Do we need to worry?* Chicago: CEMREL, 1975.

Madaus, G.F., Airasian, P.W., & Kellaghan, T. *School effectiveness: A reassessment of the evidence.* N.Y.: McGraw-Hill, in
press.

Neill, S.B. *The competency movement: Problems and solutions.*
American Association of School Administrators Critical Issues
Report. Sacramento, Calif.: Educational News Services, 1978.

Southeastern Public Education Program. *A citizen's introduction
to minimum competency programs for students.* Columbia,
S.C.: American Friends Service Committee, April, 1978.

Wirtz, W. *On further examination.* Report of the Advisory Panel
on the Scholastic Aptitude Test Score Decline. New York:
College Entrance Examination Board, 1977.

Chapter Three

Educational Measurement and Technological Bases Underlying Minimal Competency Testing

Peter W. Airasian

Introduction

If the year were 1960 and the forces promoting today's call for minimal competency testing were operating, it is likely that the response to these forces would have been quite different from today's, partly because of a changed social ethos and partly because the years intervening since 1960 have witnessed substantial changes in educational technology and measurement. The purpose of this chapter is to discuss the impact of these latter changes on the rise and practices of the minimal competency movement. In particular, three key practices in all competency testing programs—(1) defining competencies, (2) identifying suitable tests or testing procedures, and (3) setting standards to differentiate those certified as demonstrating competence from those not certified—will be explored in terms of their genesis in recent educational belief and practice. This chapter will argue that the format and procedures of minimal competency testing programs are to a large extent an outgrowth—perhaps culmination—of a series of interconnected trends which have characterized developments in and beliefs about educational measurement and technology over the past two decades. The educational technologies of 1979 are different from those of 1960, and if we are to understand the minimal competency testing movement, we must recognize not only the forces external to education which have prodded the movement into reality, but also the internal, technological features of current educational practices which influence its particular form.

Definition of Competencies

The starting point for any minimal competency testing program is an explicit specification of those knowledges, skills, and behaviors whose attainment will be taken to indicate the "competent" student. Specification of competencies in terms of student behaviors derives directly from the educational objectives movement, which first gained prominence in the 1960's. Although the idea of stating the objectives óne wished learners to obtain as a prerequisite to planning instruction and building tests had been available since the 1930's, primarily as a consequence of the writings of Ralph Tyler (1934) and his students (Bloom *et al.,* 1956), the objectives movement did not begin to dominate popular educational thinking and practice until a series of trends in the 1960's converged to make the clear specification of instructional aims take on a new and heightened importance.

Historically, the first prod to the rise of the objectives movement came from the field of educational technology. In the late 1950's and early 1960's, the use of teaching machines and programmed instruction gained a certain popularity. A central feature of most programmed instruction approaches was the identification of the terminal behavior that the learner was expected to demonstrate at the conclusion of his or her exposure to a programmed sequence of instructional elements. Indeed, since the instructional/didactic function was to be performed solely by machines, it was necessary to specify with great clarity and precision—and in terms of student behavior—both the desired end result of the instruction and the sequence of steps necessary to attain that result. The primary means of obtaining the necessary clarity and precision was to start with an explicit statement of the post-instruction behavior the learner should perform (e.g., add two-digit numbers without carrying; identify the subordinate clause in a compound sentence; etc.), and to work backwards from there, asking at each backward step, "What knowledge is prerequisite to learning the material in the step immediately prior to this one?" (Gagne, 1965). Through such a procedure, an ordered instructional sequence, derived from consideration of the desired end result of the sequence, was obtained.

The programmed instruction movement was not, in and of itself, sufficient to reorient educational practice toward explicit and clear definitions of instructional aims stated in terms of pupil behaviors. However, out of the programmed instruction movement came a very influential book written by Robert Mager, entitled *Preparing Instructional Objectives* (1962). This book provided a brief, easily followed "how to" format for stating objectives. Mager's book, in conjunction with an earlier volume on educational objectives (Bloom *et al.,* 1956), gained a wide following among curriculum developers, teachers, and evaluators. The books provided examples and sets of procedures for stating objectives that were within the power of most educators to implement.

But even the popularization of methods for stating precise educational objectives in terms of student behaviors was not sufficient to produce a rush of activity in this area. In the end, it took the federal government to tip the scale toward widespread use of educational objectives. In the early 1960's, the Department of Defense, under Robert MacNamara, was becoming increasingly beguiled by so-called rational management techniques which, in simplified form, called for a clear identification of program objectives, a charting of the stages required to meet these objectives, and an evaluation of the extent to which the objectives were ultimately attained. In today's parlance, we would term such a system a management accountability system. The ideas inherent in this accountability approach spread from the Department of Defense to education in the form of Planning-Programming-Budgeting Systems (PPBS) and HEW guidelines for program specification and evaluation.

In 1965, the Elementary and Secondary Education Act (ESEA)

was passed. By far the most comprehensive and ambitious educational Act ever envisioned in the United States, the law provided funds for local school districts to improve education, particularly for disadvantaged pupils. In the debate which accompanied the Act, concern was expressed about the possibility of providing funds to tens of thousands of local communities with no assurance that the allocated monies would result in improved education for targeted groups. After much debate, the Act was amended to include a mandate for each local district to conduct an evaluation of its program and to submit a report to the federal government. Part of this evaluation requirement, as it has evolved over the years, urges each local program to state its educational objectives. The emphasis on precisely formulated objectives defined in terms of student behaviors was quickly emulated by state education authorities, and thus, the objectives bandwagon started to roll. Title III of the Elementary and Secondary Education Act of 1965 provided funds to local districts for developing new, innovative curricula. The emphasis urged and adopted in most of these projects called for clear specification of the curriculum's objectives as a starting point for developing materials and teaching strategies. By 1970, it was hard to find an educational administrator, curriculum developer, or teacher who had not attended a workshop or a course on stating objectives, been exposed to the movement at meetings of professional organizations, or actually taken part in efforts to revamp local curricula by starting with statements of desired educational objectives.

It should be noted that the rise of the educational objectives movement was not without its thoughtful critics (Broudy, 1970; Doll, 1971; Eisner, 1969), and that a continuing debate over the merits and liabilities of precisely formulated educational objectives is in process. It is not the purpose of this discussion to chart this debate, but the reader should recognize that there is a body of opinion which is critical of the objectives movement.

The upshot of the objectives movement was a change in emphasis in teaching, curriculum planning, and evaluation. For lack of a better name, we may consider educational objectives to represent an "ends-oriented" approach to education. In such an approach, explicit formulation of the specific behavioral changes that instruction will endeavor to bring about in children assumes primacy, both temporally and conceptually. Once one has decided what he or she wishes to accomplish through instruction, that is to say, has stated the instructional objectives in unambiguous, student-oriented terms, he or she then is led to consideration of the means to be used to help learners attain these objectives. Ends precede means in this approach, and this fact, along with the explicitness with which ends must be stated, represent a change from the predominant educational practices and orientation prior to the 1960's.

The influence of the objectives movement can be observed in any number of contemporary educational approaches, including the mastery learning strategy advanced by Bloom (1968), Individually Prescribed Instructional approaches (Lindvall and Cox, 1970), and competency-based teacher education plans (Hall and Jones, 1976). Minimal competency testing programs also require the specification of precise statements about what learners can do. These statements are called minimal competencies to denote that they represent basic, fundamental capabilities all students should possess.

Measuring Competence

A second key feature in minimal competency testing programs involves the identification of measures which will be used to appraise pupil competence. There should be a logical link between the objectives one seeks learners to attain and the measures one uses to assess that attainment. The connection between objectives or competencies and measurement seems clear: the aim of measurement is to ascertain how successful one has been in attaining his or her objectives, and to do this, the measuring device one uses must reflect those objectives.

While this congruence between the ends sought and the measures used to assess whether the ends have been realized seems straightforward, it did create certain new concerns for test constructors and evaluators. Until recently, the stock in trade of educational measurers and evaluators has been the standardized, norm-referenced achievement test. While such tests are adequate for a number of purposes involving the selection of examinees in a fixed quota system where only a small number of individuals can be accommodated, they manifest two features which make them less than desirable for measuring student learning when that learning is related to a specific, well-defined set of educational objectives or competencies. First, norm-referenced tests are designed to determine an examinee's performance relative to the performance of others who have taken the test; the worth or value of an individual's score is determined not in relation to what he or she has learned but in relation to how he or she ranks in comparison to other examinees. Second, most norm-referenced tests are distributed by commercial publishing houses, which must sell a reasonably large number of them to remain economically viable. In order to obtain wide applicability for their tests, publishers tend to select rather general skills and topics which are judged to be common across a large number of textbooks or school districts.

Often, however, the general areas tapped by such tests are not reflected in the specific objectives or competencies schools seek to attain. There is, in essence, a mismatch between the objectives of instruction and the measures used to appraise student achievement; the more explicitly stated the objectives, the greater this mismatch is likely to be and the less satisfactory norm-referenced standardized tests are for evaluating student learning or competence. The rise of the objectives movement called for new kinds of measuring devices which coincided more closely with schools' precisely formulated and often divergent educational objectives; adequate tests had to be referenced to these specific objectives.

The 1960's saw three additional factors which also heightened the demand for new forms of testing (Airasian and Madaus, 1972). First, there was a growing criticism of testing, directed primarily at standardized norm-referenced tests (Hoffman, 1962; Holt, 1968). The criticism focused on concerns about the relevancy of tasks tested and the extent to which the real goals of education were reflected in multiple-choice test items. Second, there was a growing controversy surrounding grades, manifested by growing distrust of grades *per se* and a reluctance to want to judge others. Critics argued that the fight for good grades produced a competitive ethic, emphasizing "winning" the grade race at the expense of true education. Moreover, this argument concluded that—and this in many ways is the most crucial point—a grade of A or C provides no information about what a learner can *do,* only that he or she is superior or inferior to some vaguely defined reference group. Third, the late 1960's evidenced a growing belief on the part of educators that *all* or *at least most* students can learn and achieve competence in most subject areas (Bloom, 1968). Once one accepts the idea that most students can learn, the emphasis in testing shifts from one which compares pupils on a norm-referenced basis to one which measures and rewards students in terms of their performance *vis-a-vis* the objectives of instruction; if all students master the objectives, all should receive A's, passes, etc.

These factors led to the search for measuring instruments which possessed two desired properties. First, they had to reflect the specific educational objectives particular schools, teachers, or districts were seeking to foster in pupils; and second, they had to provide absolute, behaviorally specific information about pupil performance. In essence, measurement techniques had to reflect specific educational objectives, describe student learning in terms of mastery of those objectives, and permit judgments about student learning or competence which were referenced to the objectives, not to how well a pupil performed relative to other pupils.

In a paper entitled "Instructional technology and the measurement of learning outcomes," Robert Glaser (1963) introduced a distinction which, in succeeding years, was to have a major impact on educational testing and measurement. Glaser emphasized the importance of making test scores informative about pupils' behavior rather than simply about their relative attainment on the poorly specified dimensions which were assumed to lie behind test scores. Tests which provided the former type of information he called *criterion-referenced*; tests which provided information about pupil standing relative to a reference group of test-takers he termed *norm-referenced*. Glaser indicated that the score on a criterion-referenced test "provides explicit information as to what the individual can or cannot do . . . Measures which assess student achievement in terms of a criterion standard thus provide information as to the degree of competence attained by a particular student which is independent of reference to the performance of others" (pp. 519-520).

It was inevitable that the concept of criterion-referenced testing would be wedded to the objectives movement. There was, in fact, a symbiotic relation between the two: the latter encouraged specific, behavioral definitions of important learner outcomes, while the former suggested a means of linking testing to the appraisal of student learning to produce measurements that were interpretable in terms of performance on well-specified objectives. By the early 1970's, criterion-referenced testing was well ensconced in the educational lore and provided, in the judgment of many, a panacea for the solution of the measurement problems inherent in norm-referenced testing. The idea of a testing approach which referenced student performance to well-defined behavioral objectives gained widespread popularity and generated interest in a variety of similar approaches, such as domain-referenced testing (Hively, 1974), and objective-referenced testing. A more detailed review of such approaches is presented in Millman (1974). A variety of recent instructional approaches, such as Bloom's mastery learning strategy (1968), depend upon the use of tests designed to appraise student learning in terms of performance on well-specified, behaviorally stated educational objectives.

If we turn our attention back to minimal competency testing programs, it seems evident that the specific competencies (objectives) defined as important by a state or local district should be reflected in the measuring device utilized to assess student learning of the competencies. Moreover, from the point of view of remediating student failures, the measuring instruments should provide information about performance that is referenced to the competencies. While these requirements do not necessarily call for the use of criterion-referenced tests in minimal competency testing programs, they do strongly imply that criterion-referencing notions be attended to in selecting or constructing competency tests. In most states which are flirting with competency testing, a great deal of attention is being paid to the relation between the competencies desired and measurement approaches which will provide information about student performance referenced to those competencies.

Standard Setting

After defining competencies and identifying measurement procedures through which to assess learning of the competencies, most minimal competency testing programs require that a standard of performance to differentiate those to be certified competent from those not to be so certified be established. It is in providing guidance for the standard setting problem that the educational technologies and measurement procedures which have evolved over the past 20 years are of least help to the minimal competency movement. Although many people *believe* that the techniques of standard setting have evolved to the same extent as the techniques of stating objectives and building valid performance tests, this simply is not the case. Therefore, in considering what 20 years of change in educational measurement and technology imply for the standard setting problem, it is as important to identify areas of uncertainty and confusion as it is to recount specific advances.

It is clear that standards will need to be set if the aims of most minimal competency testing programs are to be realized. Regardless of whether the aim of the program is to deny some pupils a high school diploma, provide them with remedial instruction, or retain them in the same grade for an additional year, some method must be devised which will permit those demonstrating competence to be distinguished from those not demonstrating competence. It is the search for this standard or "cut-off" which has caused the greatest amount of uncertainty and controversy in minimal competency testing programs.

Part of the difficulty in standard setting can be traced to a fundamental misinterpretation of the principles of criterion-referenced testing (Glass, 1977). When Glaser coined the term 'criterion-referenced test,' the word 'criterion' referred to the behavioral referents (i.e., objectives) that the test was designed to measure. In essence, a criterion-referenced test was a test which was designed and constructed in a way which linked test performance to the specific objectives being tested. The original conception of a criterion-referenced test did *not* involve notions of performance standards and cut-off scores. Over time and with the growing use of criterion-referenced tests in the context of accountability decisions, the original conception of criterion has been corrupted to imply the setting of standards or mastery levels of student performance. In essence, a conceptualization which originally focused upon a technique for constructing and validating tests has been turned into a schema for making pass-fail, mastery-nonmastery, or "competent-incompetent" decisions. As Glass (1977) has stated in reference to this altered meaning, "It is the mathematicians and other simplifiers who prematurely translated a tentative notion . . . into the idea of cut-off scores and mastery levels. If ever there was a psychological-educational concept ill-prepared for mathematical treatment, it is the idea of criterion-referencing" (p. 14). Criterion-referenced testing, and for that matter, norm-referenced testing, do not explicitly lead to, contain, or produce standards or cut-off scores which can be used to make decisions about pupil competence or lack thereof.

Despite this fact, the word criterion is now taken by many as being synonymous with notions of standards and cut-off scores. It is necessary, therefore, to deal with the technologies and strategies which have evolved to set standards. A number of authors have identified, reviewed, or contrasted various methods of standard setting for competency testing programs (Glass, 1978; Hambleton, 1978; Jaeger, 1978; Shepard, 1976). These methods range from ones that are based upon expert consensus to ones based on empirical evidence, practical necessity, and theories of learning.

Regardless of the method considered, however, one major point regarding standard setting is critical. The setting of standards or cut-offs is arbitrary, based upon judgments (Glass, 1978). It should be noted, however, that the word "arbitrary" has two meanings. On the one hand, "arbitrary" may mean capricious; on the other hand, it may mean well-thought-out, although still judgmental. In both cases, judgment is involved, but the latter approach obviously is the more desirable (Popham, 1978). Although standard setting is often written and talked about as though it involved commonly agreed-upon, well-established procedures, such is not the case. Standards represent arbitrary judgments in two respects. First, as just noted, there are numerous methods which may be selected to establish standards. Moreover, the standards one sets using one method will not always be the same as the standards one sets using another. One must decide which of the methods will be employed, knowing that had an alternative method been selected, the standard or cut-off established might have been different. Even within a single method, as, for example, when one sets standards based upon expert judgment, different panels of experts can define different standards for the same minimal competency testing program.

The arbitrariness of standard setting extends, however, beyond the procedures selected. In minimal competency testing programs, established standards are intended to differentiate pupils who are competent from pupils who are not, pupils who can, to use the popular parlance, "function effectively" in school and society from pupils who cannot. Yet no one really knows what it means to "function effectively" in school or society, and even when one arrives at a passable definition, there are always scores of counter-examples (e.g., individuals who cannot meet the standards implied by the definition yet who, for all practical purposes, "function effectively"). The use of a single standard or cut-off score to define competence can determine only whether an individual can demonstrate competence in *that* way or at *that* level. Therefore, linking standards and standard setting to the idea of minimal competency only compounds the arbitrariness problem, since not only does one have a variety of competing methods available to set standards, but also one does not have a clear, agreed-upon, or unequivocal definition of what minimal competence means in terms of individual performance in school or society. Note that these problems arise regardless of whether one uses a norm- or a criterion-referenced minimal competency test. Some commentators argue that despite the arbitrariness problem, much is known about standard setting and that standards can and should be set (Block, 1978; Popham, 1978).

There is no question that standards *will* be set in minimal competency testing programs; they will have to be, if desired decisions about grade promotion, graduation, and remediation are to be made. What is important to bear in mind, however, is the inherent arbitrariness of the standards. There are no external criteria which one can utilize to determine empirically the appropriateness of the selected standard setting method or its relevance to pupils' effective functioning in school or society. In the end, standards are more likely to evolve and be established in concert with political realities than well-established empirical strategies.

Conclusion

This chapter has endeavored to overview recent developments in the areas of educational technology and measurement which have relevance for current-day minimal competency testing programs. The central argument made was that these developments influence the format and procedures of competency programs, and had competency programs appeared in 1960, their nature would have been quite different from present programs because educational technologies and measurement strategies have changed since 1960.

The rise of the educational objectives movement with its emphasis on describing the ends of instruction in clear, student-specific behavioral terms was considered. From the objectives movement, the conception of minimal competencies, defined as the lowest common denominator of students' education, logically derives. The rise of the criterion-referenced testing movement was also described. It was noted that the primary import of criterion-referencing relates to its potential to link student test performance to particular behavioral referents (e.g., objectives or competencies). From this notion flows a primary concern which should be recognized in selecting or constructing minimal competency tests: the tests should link student performance to the behaviors implied in the desired competencies.

Finally, the issue of standard setting was considered. It was argued that despite advances and well-defined approaches to defining competencies and building criterion-referenced tests, the problem of setting standards has not been resolved satisfactorily in the past 20 years; standard setting still rests ultimately upon judgment, and the application of different methods can produce widely divergent standards.

Overall, the growth in measurement strategies and educational technologies in the past two decades greatly colors the nature and procedures embodied in present minimal competency testing programs. The advances since 1960, however, still have left some unresolved problems and concerns in the implementation of minimal competency testing programs. In some respects, implementers cannot turn to measurement or technological advances to solve their problems. They must instead rely upon human judgment.

References

Airasian, P.W., & Madaus, G.F. Criterion-referenced testing in the classroom. *Measurement in Education,* 1972, *3,* 4, 1-8.

Block, J.H. Standards and criteria: A response. *Journal of Educational Measurement,* 1978, *15,* 4, 291-295.

Bloom, B.S. Learning for mastery. UCLA-CSEIP *Evaluation Comment,* 1968, *1.*

Bloom, B.S. *et al. Taxonomy of educational objectives, handbook 1: Cognitive domain.* N.Y.: Longman, 1956.

Broudy, H.S. Can research escape the dogma of behavioral objectives? *School Review,* 1970, *79,* 43-56.

Doll, W.E. A methodology of experience: An alternative to behavioral objectives. Paper read at the 1971 Annual Meeting of the American Educational Research Association, New York, February, 1971.

Eisner, E.W. Instructional and expressive objectives: Their formulation and use in curriculum. In *Instructional Objectives.* American Educational Research Association Monograph on

Curriculum Evaluation. Chicago: Rand McNally, 1969, 1-31.

Gagne, R.M. *The conditions of learning.* N.Y.: Holt, Rinehart, and Winston, 1965.

Glaser, R. Instructional technology and the measurement of learning outcomes. *American Psychologist,* 1963, *18,* 519-521.

Glass, G.V. Standards and criteria. Occasional Paper Number 10. Kalamazoo, Mich.: The Evaluation Center, Western Michigan University, 1977.

Glass, G.V. Standards and criteria. *Journal of Educational Measurement,* 1978, *15,* 4, 237-261.

Hall, G.E., & Jones H.L. *Competency-based education.* Englewood Cliffs, N.J.: Prentice-Hall, Inc., 1976.

Hambleton, R.K. On the use of cut-off scores with criterion-referenced tests in instructional settings. *Journal of Educational Measurement,* 1978, *15,* 4, 277-290.

Hively, W. Introduction to domain-referenced testing. *Educational Technology,* 1974, *14,* 5-10.

Hoffman, B. *The tyranny of testing.* N.Y.: Collier Books, 1962.

Holt, J.W. *On testing.* Cambridge, Mass.: Pinck Leodas Assoc., 1968.

Jaeger, R.M. A proposal for setting a standard on the North Carolina high school competency test. Paper presented at the 1978 Spring meeting of the North Carolina Association for Research in Education, Chapel Hill, North Carolina, 1978.

Lindvall, C.M., & Cox, R. *Evaluation as a tool in curriculum development: The IPI evaluation program.* American Educational Research Association Monograph Series on Curriculum Evaluation. Chicago: Rand McNally, 1970.

Mager, R.F. *Preparing instructional objectives.* Palo Alto, Calif.: Fearon Publishers, 1962.

Millman, J. Criterion-referenced measurement. In W.J. Popham (Ed.), *Evaluation in education.* Berkeley, Calif.: McCutchan Publishing Co., 1974, 309-397.

Popham, W.J. *Criterion-referenced measurement.* Englewood Cliffs, N.J.: Prentice-Hall, 1978.

Popham, W.J. As always, provocative. *Journal of Educational Measurement,* 1978, *15,* 4, 297-300.

Shepard, L.A. Setting standards and living with them. Paper presented at the 1976 meeting of the National Council on Measurement in Education, San Francisco, California, April, 1976.

Tyler, R.W. *Constructing achievement tests.* Columbus: Ohio State Press, 1934.

Chapter Four

Making Sense of the Competency Testing Movement *

Walt Haney
George F. Madaus

The minimal competency testing movement is a peculiar phenomenon. According to the Education Commission of the States (ECS), which has assumed the role of chronicler of the competency testing movement, a majority of the 50 states has already mandated some sort of competency testing—either through legislation or via action by state boards of education (Pipho, 1978a, 1978b). The ECS reports, "Minimal competency testing for high school graduation and grade-to-grade promotion continues to be one of the most explosive issues on the educational scene today" (Pipho, 1977, p.i). In short, this kind of testing represents a major movement with serious implications for American education. Yet, this sudden enthusiasm for competency testing poses a contradiction, for it comes just at a time when more and more questions are being raised about, and criticisms leveled against, tests and test use generally.

*From *Harvard Educational Review,* 1978, *49,* 4, 462-484. Edited, abridged, and reprinted with permission of authors and publisher. Copyright © 1978 The President and Fellows of Harvard College.

A great deal of attention has recently been given to the details of how minimal competency testing schemes can be implemented. Yet, too often, enthusiasts of minimal competency testing seem inclined to rush into implementation without considering the ambiguities involving the ideas on which such testing programs are based. What are these things called competencies? Can practical minimal competencies be defined? Do we know how to test for them? In this chapter, we argue that the enthusiasm for competency testing cannot be explained in terms of clear answers to such questions. Instead, we must search for an explanation in the historical and political issues that appear to have inspired the competency testing movement. Such factors, we find, help to explain current concern over the quality of schooling, but they still do not account for the enthusiasm for testing as such. The emphasis on testing seems to fit with certain structural features of American education, which may lead, we argue, to the questionable testing of undefined competencies based on arbitrarily defined minimums. In the conclusion, we draw attention to the major problems we foresee in minimal competency testing and suggest some antidotes to possible unintended consequences of such programs.

What Is Competency Testing?

The enthusiasm for competency tests stems from a belief that the testing of essential skills and competencies will help raise academic standards and increase educational achievement. The idea is that requiring certification of competencies will prevent schools from passing incompetent students through the grades simply on the basis of social promotion. Among the variety of competency testing schemes now being discussed or implemented there are two main forms: controlling grade-to-grade promotion, and providing a minimum basis for awarding high school diplomas. The issues are somewhat different in each of these. Here, we concentrate primarily on the use of competency testing as a prerequisite for high school graduation, although many of the issues we raise are also pertinent to competency testing for grade promotion.

There is one important point to note at the outset. Interest in competency testing has focused almost exclusively on *minimal* competencies. A recent report on competency-based education in Oregon, for example, noted that "the heart of a competency-based education program is the identification of the minimum abilities each student must attain in order to function in society" (U.S. Congress, 1977, p. 243). This easy equation of competencies with minimal abilities is questionable. Thomas Green (1977) has argued that policy goals are always minimal standards because "they operate as measures of failure rather than as standards of success" (p. 3). This connection is arguable, although recent experience seems to support Green's assertion. Competency tests more frequently than not seem to have become minimal competency tests.

On the surface, the idea of minimal competency testing is immensely attractive. How can anyone possibly argue against "competence"? In a time of widespread concern over deteriorating educational standards, fueled by declining SAT scores, systematic assessment of students' competence certainly seems to make sense. (SAT scores do not, of course, measure minimal competencies.) Students who are certified minimally competent avoid the suspicion that they are products of a faltering educational system, and students who fail competency tests can theoretically receive remedial help in order to gain the competencies and skills they need to enter the world of work.

If one assumes that minimal competency testing is a plausible means of bolstering educational standards, many questions arise regarding implementation. Discussions at four regional conferences on minimal competency testing in the fall of 1977, sponsored by the ECS, the National Institute of Education, and the Carnegie Corporation of New York, focused on the following questions:

- What competencies will you require?
- How will you measure them?
- When will you measure them?
- How many minimums will be established?
- How high will the minimums be set?
- Will minimums be set for schools, or for students?

• What will be done with those who do not pass the competency tests? (Brickell, 1978).

In several important respects, however, these questions take far too much for granted. They assume that minimal competency testing is a plausible tool for bolstering educational achievement, but they ignore the fact that adequate means to implement such schemes may simply not be available. As Glass (1977) has remarked, "A common expression of wishful thinking is to base a grand scheme on a fundamental unresolved problem." There are three such unresolved problems concerning minimal competency testing programs: the definition of competencies, the specification of minimal competencies, and the testing of minimal competencies.

Competencies. The symbolic function of the term "competencies" is substantial. One synonym for competency is ability, but given the poor public standing of ability testing nowadays, a minimal ability testing movement would probably not get very far. So, while the symbolic function of the term "competency" is substantial, its exact meaning is unclear. Sometimes it seems to be used according to one of its dictionary definitions, "sufficient means for a modest livelihood": all students should have sufficient means for a modest livelihood by the time they leave high school. Often it seems to connote broad abilities to get along in late twentieth century America: hence, we find allusions, as in the Oregon competency-based education program, to the abilities each student must attain "in order to function in society." Elsewhere in the minimal competency testing literature we find references to "life skills," "essential skills," or "survival skills." Yet skills comprise only part of the aims of education. As MacDonald-Ross (1973) has observed:

> It is easy to find types of educational experiences which have nothing to do with skills—learning for learning's sake, for instance. The distinction between knowledge and skills is deeply embedded in our ordinary language for the excellent reason that it is meaningful and functionally necessary. To have a skill is to have the ability to execute useful tasks to publicly agreed standards of performance (p. 29).

Thus, the language of minimal competency testing suggests

concern, not with the broader goals of education, but more narrowly with the issue of skill acquisition.

Discussions often proceed as if competencies or skills can be easily identified. Efforts have been made to use experts or "objective analysis" to determine those skills needed by adults to "function" or to "survive" in society. These efforts have resulted in very detailed specifications of competencies and life skills. But brief reflection suggests that the meaning of minimal functioning in society is very hard to pin down. People function differently in society, and some do in ways offensive to others. Even if we could reach agreement on what constitutes success (say, functioning at a high level of competency) and what constitutes minimal functioning in society, their determinants are simply not very well understood. We do know, for example, that success in school seems not to be a good predictor of success in later life—at least as measured by social scientists. So, perhaps skills taught in preparation for passing competency tests will be of little value later on.

Since some "life skills"—for example, filling out tax forms or looking something up in the Yellow Pages—are not directly taught in many schools, it might be unfair to deny someone a high school diploma for lack of proficiency in skills not taught in school. A fundamental issue in the competency testing movement, then, is whether to assess competencies that will be needed later in life or restrict testing to the more traditional school skills, on the assumption that they have some relationship to success beyond school.

The latter approach seems to have been the one adopted by most states planning minimal competency testing. According to a recent ECS summary, 17 states have mandated some sort of competency testing connected to high school graduation, and several others are considering it. Such schemes give attention mainly to skills in reading, writing, and arithmetic. In only a handful of states do skill areas tested for high school graduation go beyond those three. In some states, students are required to demonstrate those skills in applied situations or in terms of functional literacy.

The tactic of focusing on testing in school skills has, however, been criticized as misleading:

> It's like the bait-and-switch advertising tactic, in which at the point of sale an inferior item or less attractive product is substituted for the more desirable item. The attractive product is an education that develops competencies needed for life. . . . The switched product in the bait-and-switch swindle is a score on a standardized paper-and-pencil competency examination. It is a poor substitute for the real thing: performance at life's tasks (Nathan and Jennings, 1978, pp. 621-622).

There is little scientific basis to support the idea that we know what the important skills are, and the tests that presume to assess these competencies cannot withstand serious scrutiny of their ability to predict competency in life skills, survival, or functioning.

Minimums. Agreement on what desirable areas of competence might be—Oregon, for example, requires competencies in six life-roles with 20 required areas of study—may be considerably easier to establish than the cut-off point for minimal competency. In a recent paper, Gene Glass examined six different methods of determining cut-off scores, and he concluded that alternative methods can result in markedly different proportions of various populations reaching the desired standard. So far as he knows, "every attempt to derive a criterion score [for example, to define minimal competency] is either blatantly arbitrary or derives from a set of arbitrary premises" (Glass, 1977, p. 42). In 1977, the Educational Testing Service (ETS) published the *Manual for Setting Standards on the Basic Skills Assessment Tests* (Zieky and Livingston, 1977). In reviewing the ETS manual, Glass (1978) charges that the "authors are guilty of every non sequitur, every solecism, and wrong thought" (p. 604) he had warned against in his earlier paper. If the value judgments underlying the setting of a cut-off score are clearly recognized, then statistical techniques can help reduce error in determining whether a student reached the cut-off point or not. But the matter to be kept in mind (and the matter about which Glass and the ETS authors are unequally worried) is that elaborate statistical techniques cannot do away with the subjectivity involved in setting cut-off scores.

In practice, the setting of minimal scores seems to be the result of compromise between judgments of what minimums seem plausible to expect and judgments about what proportions of failure seem politically tolerable. In New York, for example, discussions of proposed minimal competencies focused on arguments that the tests proposed were too easy and would pull the curriculum down. The idea of minimal competency tests as a requirement for high school graduation was first approved by the New York State Board of Regents in March, 1976. The initial plan was that tests in reading and mathematics would go into effect in 1977, and tests in civics, health, and writing would begin in 1980. When ninth-grade-equivalent achievement was proposed as an appropriate minimal level to be required for high school graduation, one official in the mayor's office (apparently without any understanding of grade-equivalent scores) responded, "What happened to the twelfth grade?" Board of Regents member Kenneth Clark described the New York standards as "embarrassingly too low." When the initially proposed tests were criticized as "ridiculously easy," a new set of tests was mandated by the Board to take effect in 1981. Recently, the Deputy Mayor of New York expressed the view that competency standards could be further upgraded by keeping slow learners back in the early grades and giving them special tutoring ("Educator is critical of competency tests," 1977; "Ideas and trends in summary," 1978; "Regents block tests as too easy," 1978; "Regents replacing competency tests," 1978; "Regents toughening high school exams," 1978).

In Connecticut, similar reactions were reported. When a seventh-grade-equivalent reading level was proposed as a minimal condition for high school graduation, the school board was charged with misrepresentation: "We're paying for 12 years of schooling, but we're only getting seven years" (Nathan and Jennings, 1978, p. 624).

Such responses bring up another problem in setting minimums, and one that is likely to become more and more important—namely, the consequence of setting a minimum at a particular level. If, as the above criticisms suggest, a minimum level of twelfth-grade-equivalent performance were required, around 50 percent of the twelfth graders could be expected to fail—simply because of the way grade-equivalent scores are calculated. This example is unrealistic, but it does illustrate what seems to be a common experience. Standards that are established on a common-sense basis frequently result in a considerably higher than expected proportion of students failing to meet them. In Florida, for example, when the mathematics portion of a state-wide proficiency examination was administered to high school juniors in the fall of 1977, 40-50 percent failed. Florida's Commissioner of Education had predicted that only one-quarter to one-third might fail ("Math a big problem for Florida schools," 1977). At present, there simply is no scientific foundation for deciding what "minimum" points should be; the decisions involved in setting them are political rather than scientific.

Testing. Failure rates on initial proficiency examinations that are higher than expected add to the alarm over faltering educational standards. *The New York Times* called the results of the Florida mathematics-proficiency examination "new evidence that Johnny, the celebrated nonreader, also cannot add, subtract, or divide" ("Math a big problem for Florida schools," 1977). In the same week, *Time* magazine ran an article on the Florida results under the headline "Florida Flunks."

Later accounts suggested that the high rates of failure in Florida represented more than just failure of students to learn what they were taught. Subsequent news articles noted that some high school juniors considered by teachers to be among their best students had failed the proficiency examination. In explanation, one person pointed out that "there are algebra students who haven't worked with decimals for a long time. Some kids have never figured a sales tax. That, coupled with reading things into questions, can make a student fail" ("Good pupils fail Florida test," 1977). In other words, the problem may in some cases be that minimal competency tests are not measuring what students have been taught—or, at least, not what they have been taught recently. If this is true, then the validity of the inferences made from the competency tests must be called into question.

This issue is similar to that encountered in studies of school effectiveness. For example, the validity of the now famous inference by Coleman, Campbell, Hobson, McPartland, Mood, Weinfeld, and York (1966) that "schools bring little to bear on a child's achievement that is independent of his background and general social context" (p. 325) ultimately depends on the appropriateness of the measures they used to test school effectiveness. A strong argument can be made that the tests they used did not measure school achievement at all; they measured general verbal ability, which in turn is a surrogate for home background. Coleman's tests were not sensitive to what was actually taught in the schools, particularly at the secondary level (Madaus, Airasian, Kellaghan, in press).

Minimal competency tests should measure topics actually covered in the school curriculum. This issue may be especially pertinent to life-skills tests because some of those skills may not be taught in school. In addition, minimal competency tests may have to be instructionally valid—that is, topics in the curriculum must actually have been taught to the students tested (McClung, 1977). For example, assuming that a student has been instructed in reading, would a test that required reading in a format not directly included in the school curriculum—say, in classified advertisements (as in a life-skills competency test)—be instructionally valid? How about a test in which the format was the same as in school material, but which included vocabulary not taught in school?

Other forms of measurement validity will also have to be considered. Do minimal competency tests have adequate construct and content validity in terms of the competencies they supposedly test? Further, if a minimal competency testing scheme is aimed at measuring not just academic skills, but also life skills, the predictive validity of the tests in terms of life skills will also be a relevant issue. Other questions are whether minimal competency tests are a reliable means for making decisions about individual students, and whether they can be made free of cultural and sexual bias.

As soon as the important consequences begin to flow from any minimal competency testing program, legal challenges are certain to follow. Precedent has already been established for bringing suit on issues such as test validity (Lerner, 1978). The cost implications of testing are likely to arouse concern as well (Airasian, Madaus, and Pedulla, 1978).

Consider only the problems of test development and the measurement procedure. For some life-skills competencies (for example, filling out a tax form), it is possible to conceive of reasonable performance tests, though the development of standardized procedures for validating, administering, and scoring such tests is likely to be expensive. For others that are more complex, it is considerably more difficult. Development of new tests and concepts of competence would require a serious and sustained effort, with no guarantee of success. In fact, the experience of competence testers will likely duplicate that of program evaluators in the past. They start with the hope of mounting broad, truly comprehensive assessments, and after spending a great deal of time and money, end up with disappointment. One example is the effort of the national Follow Through evaluation team to develop new instruments for the measurement of a broad range of educational goals. One member of that evaluation contractor's staff reported, "The money that was spent on the development of non-cognitive measures was wasted. Period" (see Haney, 1977, p. 183).

The problems of test development and its cost have led some states and localities simply to adopt commercially available tests of reading and mathematics as their initial competence assessment devices. In Florida, for example, items from the Adult Performance Level Test and others developed by ETS, have been used (Fisher, 1978; McClung, 1977), a practice that raises a number of validity issues. Imposition of readily available tests can very easily come to define skills taught, rather than desired skills guiding the selection of appropriate assessment instruments.

Despite widespread discussion of minimal competency testing, surprisingly little attention has been given to the character of the tests themselves. The few samples of minimal competency tests that are available suggest that, despite their name, most of them follow the old familiar format: multiple-choice, true-false, or short answer. Instead of having students perform certain tasks in order to demonstrate their competencies (as, for example, in the road-test part of the driver's license examination), these tests assess competencies indirectly via paper-and-pencil tests that are presumed to correlate with the competencies of real interest. In assessing competency for high school graduation, for example, districts often do not require students to write anything; instead, they are asked via a multiple-choice format to identify mistakes in a writing sample that is provided. The prime virtue of these indirect forms of assessment is that they are cheap both to administer and to score; in addition, they have been justified in terms of their power to predict subsequent achievement. French (1966), for example, reports that multiple-choice tests of verbal aptitude can "predict English grades or ratings on writing ability better than a test which actually requires the students to write" (p. 587).

There are several counter-arguments to such claims. Standardized multiple-choice tests of writing like the STEP writing test, despite French's claim, have very low correlation with direct measures of writing (Madaus and Rippey, 1960). More importantly, justifying machine-scorable test instruments in terms of their power to predict school achievement belies the whole rationale of minimal competency testing. The rationale behind the movement is that it will help guarantee competencies for life after school, not for life in school. Even if one were to accept such arguments, minimal competency testing has taken hold so rapidly and tests have been developed so quickly that it is quite unlikely that evidence of such predictive validity is available for most of these tests.

The problems inherent in specifying life-skills competencies, setting minimums for those competencies, and testing the degree to which individuals possess them seem truly formidable. For the list of competencies already specified in several states, no good measuring instruments are available, and even in those domains where we do have measurement devices, validity and reliability may simply not be sufficient to provide adequate grounds for withholding a high school diploma. It seems clear that if the enthusiasm for minimal competency testing were a direct reflection of our competence to create such tests, the movement would be more mole-hill than mountain.

The History and Politics of Minimal Competency Testing

But the enthusiasm is as great as the scientific foundations are shaky. If we are to explain the popularity of minimal competency testing, we have to look elsewhere. One obvious source of enthusiasm is the notion that schools need more scientific management. Minimal competency testing is simply the latest verse in this old refrain—one that goes back at least a century. In 1877, the New York State Legislature empowered the Regents to institute a system of examinations "to furnish a suitable standard of graduation" (Spaulding, 1938). Around the turn of the century, Josiah Rice, E.L. Thorndike, and scores of others recommended more thorough measurement of school results in order to modernize and improve education. One enthusiast of scientific management for the schools at that time said, "We may not hope to achieve progress except as . . . measuring sticks are available or may be derived" (quoted by Callahan, 1962, p. 101).

Despite past experience, similar views on reforming American schools have been presented recently under a variety of new labels: systems analysis, planning-programming-budgeting systems, and cost-benefit analysis, to name just a few. The theme behind all of these ideas is that more systematic management of education can improve results. The trouble with these proposals, most of them modeled after industrial practices, is that they overlook the greater complexity of schools and education. In industry, management can rationalize its procedures because it is clear about the ends it seeks and has close control over the means of production. Neither of these conditions is present in the schools, and as a result, not surprisingly, none of the technological approaches to educational management have been very successful. But, although it is difficult to account for the popularity of minimal competency testing in terms of past successes, it does seem to reflect the durability of the idea that science can improve the efficiency of schools.

Another explanation is the windshift in prevailing political weather—from liberal to conservative thinking on education. Different observers use different labels to identify the change: some call it a shift from concern over equality to concern over excellence; some refer to a shift from educational equity to educational achievement. Harold Howe, in his keynote address to a recent HEW-sponsored conference on achievement testing and the basic skills, said, "It seems probable that some erosion in school services to the general population may have been the price of moving toward equality of educational opportunity for those who have so long been denied it" (Howe, 1978, p. 6). In large part, the minimal competency testing movement seems to have grown out of such perceptions and the politics flowing from them; doubtless, the emphasis on minimal competency helped to make the movement politically more palatable. One suspects, for example, that little enthusiasm would greet competency testing if all students were to be graded, from say, one to 100, instead of only marked pass-fail.

The political perspective helps explain why there has been so little concern over the emphasis on "basic skills." Enthusiasts of competency testing seem little worried about focusing initially on reading, writing, and mathematics, because they often see a need for more work in just those "basics" and for ending the practice of routine promotion. In part, the minimal competency movement is one aspect of the "back to basics" movement, which in turn is part of a backlash to the "funsie-wunsie open education" philosophy of the 1960's (Kilpatrick, 1977). This reaction against "new-fangled education" as Kilpatrick puts it harks back to "old-fashioned" education, often overlooking the difference that old-fashioned education served a much smaller proportion of the population than schools now serve.

In 1940, less than half of the adult population of the United States had ever even begun high school. By 1975, around 90 percent of the adult population had completed 12 or more years of schooling (Golladay, 1977, p. 212). Although nostalgia for times past—or a sense of loss, as Cohen (1976) put it—may help to explain the enthusiasm for competency testing, it also often seems to ignore the realities of the present. Interestingly, despite the widespread sense of diminishing educational standards, there is some evidence that in the last 30 years learning may not actually have diminished. A study comparing the reading achievement of

Indiana school children in 1944 and 1976 found that today's students generally do as well as, or better than, their counterparts in 1944 when the exact same test used in 1944 was readministered in 1976 (Farr, Fay, and Negley, 1978).

Why the Focus on Testing?

These explanations of the growth of the minimal competency movement make sense, but they are not complete. The movement is part of a much broader national reemphasis on improving educational achievement in basic skills, but why has it taken the form of calls for more testing, rather than just more schooling? In the 1950's, a similar concern over educational quality led, not to minimal competency tests, but to more direct efforts to reform curricula. Why curriculum reform in the 1950's, but minimal competency testing in the 1970's?

The focus on testing perhaps stems in part from the fact that it is reform from afar. It "is clearly being led, or pushed, by non-educators" (Pipho, 1978a, p. 586). As non-educators, enthusiasts of competency testing are free to focus on the results and to pay little heed to the processes by which they might be achieved. Yet more thoughtful specialists in educational measurement have long pointed out that such myopia may be misleading. As Samuel Messick wrote in 1975: "To judge the value of an outcome or end, one should understand the nature of the processes or means that led to that end, as Dewey (1939) emphasized in his principle of the means-end continuum: it's not just that means are appraised in terms of the ends they lead to, but ends are appraised in terms of the means that produce them (p. 963)." The influence of non-educators in reforming education is noteworthy but not especially new. As Raymond Callahan noted in 1962 in *Education and the Cult of Efficiency,* the vulnerability of American education to external pressures has a fairly long history.

Another angle on the current phenomenon is rising public concern over the costs of education. Public education is by far the largest and most expensive undertaking of state and local governments, accounting for more than one-third of their direct expenditures. Local school districts, on the average, receive about

50 percent of their total revenues from local taxes, most of it from property taxes. Over the past decade, per pupil expenditures have increased more than 50 percent, even after adjusting for inflation. Dissatisfaction over the escalation of costs is reflected in the marked nationwide drop both in the number of school-bond elections and in the proportion of elections where bond sales were approved—from 74 percent in 1964-65 to 46 percent in 1974-75 (Golladay, 1977). Not only is the public apparently reluctant to pay more, but it is increasingly demanding proof of the return on the expenditures it is already making. Since test scores are the handiest measure of educational performance we have, such demands more often than not get translated into calls for more testing.

Added to the influence of the public and to costs is the shift in patterns of school governance over the last several decades (Cohen, 1978). While formal governance arrangements vest authority for education in local and state education agencies, authority has gradually been accumulating in the hands of agencies and organizations that cut across local and state boundaries—teachers unions, the courts, testing agencies, and a range of other educational lobby groups. The hands of local agencies are increasingly tied—by collective-bargaining contracts, the federal government, and court orders.

Governance of education has, in effect, become far more complex since the 1950's and far more national—or at least supra-local—in character, so public concern over the direction it is taking gets expressed in different ways as well. Both tradition and law preclude direct federal intervention in educational curricula, and in most states determination of curricula is the clear prerogative of local education agencies. Mandates for minimal competency testing at the state level seem to fit well with the *de facto* allocation of responsibility for education across the three levels of government. State governments can mandate minimal competency testing without infringing—at least directly—on the local responsibility for curriculum. Federal agencies are kept at bay—at least ostensibly—because a national test would represent too much of an intervention into state and local responsibilities for education. Instead, they can get in on the action by providing funding and technical assistance to states and localities considering minimal competency testing, by sponsoring conferences and research, and by other similarly indirect means.

The minimal competency testing movement at the state level fits well with the current mix of government responsibilities for education and with private interests as well. Test companies, for example, see a windfall in helping states and localities develop tests, and a multitude of experts and consulting firms are already doing a brisk business in proffering advice on techniques and options.

In the end, of course, it is impossible to know exactly why a movement like minimal competency testing finds public favor. The rapid rise of the minimal competency testing movement seems due largely to the fact that so many diverse interests converge on the idea. Conservatives support it because of concerns over costs; liberals favor it to promote more quality education for all children. What remains to be seen is the influence this movement will have on the lives and learning of children themselves. Educational fads and movements doubtless have more impact on public discourse and media coverage of education than on classroom practice: indeed, the appetites of education experts, consultants, and journalists seem to demand a new issue every three or four years. Yet, since minimal competency testing has already attained the status of law in large portions of the country, it may well have a more lasting effect on teachers and students than some of the other recent accountability schemes.

What to Look for in Minimal Competency Testing

Forecasting the future of minimal competency testing seems as uncertain as reading tea leaves. In a meeting in May, 1978, Florida officials predicted that their state's minimal competency testing program was a harbinger: it would be adopted in other states sooner than educators expect ("Florida's minimum competency testing," 1978). In the same month, however, Glass predicted in *Phi Delta Kappan* that Florida's minimal competency graduation assessment "will be suspended before the end of the year" (p.

603). Airasian, Madaus, and Pedulla (1978) observed that the movement seemed to be heading toward something like European practices of external certification for secondary school graduation; how far we will go in that direction is hard to predict.

A plague of prognosticators has been at work predicting what the future will or should hold for minimal competency testing; Gene Glass and the Florida State Department of Education officials represent opposite ends of the spectrum of opinion. The National Association of Secondary School Principals predicted eight possible positive results and eight possible negative ones (1976, p. 14). The American Friends Service Committee, in *A Citizen's Introduction to Minimum Competency Programs,* saw four potential benefits and seven potential problems (Southeastern Public Education Program, 1978). The Education Commission of the States recently adopted a set of eight policy recommendations concerning such testing, dealing as much with institutional territoriality on the minimal competency testing issue as with substantive educational concerns. In brief, the ECS recommendations are: (1) states and local districts should adopt a comprehensive plan for setting standards and for establishing criteria for determining when those standards have been met; (2) the purpose for the testing and standards should be clearly determined; (3) diagnosis of why pupils do not attain minimal standards and how to remedy those deficiencies should be components of any minimal competency program; (4) the federal government should not become involved in minimal competency testing in states or establish a national testing program or national minimal competency standards; (5) the procedures and processes for developing and implementing standards should encourage active involvement among all concerned groups; (6) careful attention must be given not only to the content and administration of the test, but also to the provision of compensatory and bilingual education programs, remediation, and any other instructional strategies necessary to ensure that application of the standards will not discriminate against minorities or the disadvantaged; (7) development of minimal competency tests and administration of minimal competency standards cost money; sufficient funds should be provided to develop and implement them well; and (8) policy-makers should give attention to ways in which the expertise located in institutions of higher education can be used in implementing a minimal competency program (ECS, 1978).

Some organizations with similar constituencies—the National Education Association and the American Federation of Teachers, the National Association of Elementary School Principals, and the National Association of Secondary School Principals, for example—seem to have taken markedly different positions on the minimal competency testing issue. Why such differences appear is unclear. Do they reflect different educational philosophies or different political interests?

In our view, the problems inherent in minimal competency testing are more obvious than the benefits, and perhaps this is the reason that state action concerning minimal competency testing slowed somewhat in 1978.

> What is noticeable this year is that the legislatures are moving much more carefully. They are holding more hearings; they are reviewing bills in greater detail; they are giving more consideration to additional studies when needed; in general, they are asking more questions. At the state board level, several states are working through elaborate schedules of state-wide hearings and involving all groups through advisory boards before adopting policy. Even after policy has been set, provisions are made for a period of review before it becomes final (Pipho, 1978a, p. 585).

But though action is slowing, interest remains high. The idea behind minimal competency testing still seems reasonable. These tests, it is hoped, will help guarantee that students no longer automatically pass through schools simply on the basis of social promotion. Competency testing schemes try to ensure that in return for the time spent in schools, students will be guaranteed some minimum amount of learning, in terms either of "school skills" or "life competencies." The idea is a natural extension of other current themes of social policy and legislation—minimum wages, environmental quality, and minimally adequate health care. Though the American public seems increasingly concerned with the costs of these social-welfare guarantees, its enchantment with them does not otherwise seem to be waning. So it is with minimal competency testing: the idea still seems attractive; it is the connection between theory and practice that is worrisome.

In this respect, some issues seem especially important. More attention needs to be given to the relationship between minimal competency testing and what is being taught in the schools. In the rush to test for competencies, remarkably little attention has been given to how the competencies or skills tested relate to present school curricula. The match between what is tested and what is taught needs considerably more attention.

If the educational goals embodied in competency testing schemes are not adequately covered in current curricula, the discrepancy needs resolution. Testing students on what they have not been taught is unfair, and denying them a high school diploma on that basis may well prove to be illegal. If the fit between what is tested and what is taught is not good, testing will also affect the curriculum. Experience with programs using tests to certify successful completion of a given level of education shows that examinations quickly influence what is and is not taught, how it is taught, and how pupils study (Madaus and MacNamara, 1970). If students are denied a high school diploma on the basis of minimal competency examinations, these tests could quickly become a powerful influence on what is taught and learned in American schools.

Most minimal competency testing programs quite sensibly have not waited until the twelfth grade to administer tests to students. Students are usually given several chances to pass them, beginning early in their high school careers. Relatively little attention has been given, however, to the issue of the sort of remedial help that will be given to students who do not pass the first time around. Florida is again prototypical of this problem. Only after nearly 40 percent of eleventh graders taking the mathematics proficiency test failed did the state "provide a compensatory education program that this year distributed $10 million to local districts (on the basis of state assessment scores) to provide remedial instruction" (Fisher, 1978, p. 601).

The availability of well-thought-out remediation efforts on a broad scale—and our experience with compensatory education at the elementary level should give us pause here—will be crucial in determining whether minimal competency testing programs really help to improve education. If not, they may simply supply a new means for tracking students who most need help into second-class educational programs and stigmatizing them as inferior citizens.

Disadvantaged students, including minorities, handicapped children, and students who do not speak English as their first language typically have not had educational opportunities equivalent to those of their middle-class peers. The potential of minimal competency tests for adverse impact on these groups is great. Already this issue has been raised in several southern states. In North Carolina, a boycott of the state-wide competency test has been advocated by minority leaders ("Competency test boycott proposed," 1978). In Florida, the NAACP has announced its intention to file suit to enjoin further administration of Florida's proficiency examination on the grounds that it is culturally biased ("Florida NAACP," 1978). Regardless of whether the tests themselves are biased or whether minorities have received inferior instruction, the potential for discrimination seems great. A recent Southern Regional Council report suggested that tracking based on competency test results may become the new segregation (Mills and Bryan, 1976).

Airasian, Madaus, and Pedulla (1978) observed that one problem little noted in discussions of minimal competency testing is the issue of test security. Some minimal competency tests are modeled after the SAT, the Law School Admissions Tests, and other completely secure tests. The same tests, or large portions of them, are used year after year and are never made public. For tests such as the SAT and the LSAT, this approach makes some sense; individuals voluntarily take the test and pay the examining body a fee for the services they provide in making up and administering them.

The completely secure model of testing does not, however, seem appropriate for minimal competency testing. First of all, students will not take such tests voluntarily; instead, they will be required to do so. Second, the tests are being developed with public monies, and freedom-of-information laws may require that they be made public after they have been administered. If they are, test security will vanish, and new tests will have to be developed for each administration. External testing programs tied to high school certification have in the past followed this procedure rather than the totally secure approach of the SAT. Following this tack will, however, increase the cost of a minimal competency testing program, because test development will not be a one-shot affair (Airasian, Madaus, and Pedulla, 1978).

The problems of implementing minimal competency testing programs appear at present to be far larger than the benefits derived from them. The major problems arise from the relationship between what these tests measure and what is actually taught in schools. This relationship, or lack of it, deserves considerably more attention than it has so far received. If the relationship is weak, the tests are unfair; if it is strong, it may be because what is tested affects what is taught. Competency testing schemes may have real, though unintended, consequences, both for students and for the substance of what gets taught in school. The most sensible antidote to such unintended consequences is to devote more attention to what should be taught in the schools and how to teach it more effectively and less on merely that which conveniently can be measured. For the maximum of what currently can be measured, especially using paper-and-pencil competency tests, should not define the minimum of what is taught or learned.

References

Airasian, P., Madaus, G., & Pedulla, J. *Issues in minimal competency testing and a comparison of implementation models* (Report to the Policy Subcommittee of the Massachusetts Advisory Committee on High School Graduation Requirements). Chestnut Hill, Mass.: Boston College, April, 1978.

Brickell, H. *Let's talk about . . . minimum competency testing.* Denver, Colo.: Education Commission of the States, 1978.

Callahan, R. *Education and the cult of efficiency.* Chicago, Ill.: University of Chicago Press, 1962.

Cohen, D.K. Loss as a theme in social policy. *Harvard Educational Review,* 1976, *46,* 553-571.

Cohen, D.K. Reforming school politics. *Harvard Educational Review,* 1978, *48,* 429-447.

Coleman, J.S., Campbell, E.Q., Hobson, C.J., McPartland, J., Mood, A., Weinfeld, F.D., & York, R.L. *Equality of educational opportunity.* Washington, D.C.: U.S. Government Printing Office, 1966.

Competency test boycott proposed. *Chatham County Herald,* July 19, 1978.

Dewey, J. Theory of valuation. In O. Neuroth, R. Carnap, and C. Morris (Eds.), *International encyclopedia of unified science* (Vol. 2). Chicago: University of Chicago Press, 1939.

Education Commission of the States. *Policy issues in minimum competency standards and testing* (draft). Denver, Colo.: Author, 1978.

Educator is critical of competency tests. *The New York Times,* November 20, 1977.

Farr, R., Fay, L., & Negley, H. Then and now: Reading achievement in Indiana (1944-45 and 1976). Unpublished manuscript, Indiana University, School of Education, 1978.

Fisher, T.H. Florida's approach to competency testing. *Phi Delta Kappan,* 1978, *59,* 599-602.

Florida flunks. *Time,* December 12, 1977.

Florida's minimum competency testing: Is it coming or going? *Report on Education Research,* May 17, 1978.

Florida NAACP will sue state education officials over literacy tests. *Education Daily,* March 29, 1978.

French, J.W. Schools of thought in judging excellence in English themes. In A. Anastasi (Ed.), *Testing problems in perspective.* Washington, D.C.: American Council on Education, 1966.

Glass, G. Standards and criteria (Occasional Paper Series of the Evaluation Center). Unpublished manuscript, Western Michigan University, December, 1977.

Glass, G. Minimum competence and incompetence in Florida. *Phi Delta Kappan,* 1978, *59,* 602-605.

Golladay, M. *The condition of education 1977* (Stock No. 017-080-01678-8). Washington, D.C.: U.S. Government Printing Office, 1977.

Good pupils fail Florida test. *Washington Post,* December, 1977.

Green, T. *Minimal educational standards: A systematic perspective.* Background paper prepared for the Education Commission of the States/National Institute of Education/Carnegie Corporation Regional Conference on Minimum Competency Testing, 1977.

Haney, W. *A technical history of the national Follow Through evaluation.* Cambridge, Mass.: Huron Institute, 1977. (Also issued by the U.S. Office of Education and The Follow Through Evaluation, Vol. V of the Follow Through Planned Variation Experiment Series.)

Howe, H. *Tests and schooling.* Address to the National Conference on Achievement Testing and the Basic Skills, Washington, D.C., March, 1978.

Ideas and trends in summary. *The New York Times,* June 6, 1978.

Kilpatrick, J. Teaching by the book pays off. *Denver Post,* June 28, 1977.

Lerner, B. Equal protection and external screening: Davis, DeFunis, and Bakke. In *Education, measurement, and the law, Proceedings of the 1977 ETS Invitational Conference.* Princeton, N.J.: Educational Testing Service, 1978.

MacDonald-Ross, M. Behavioral objectives—A critical review. *Industrial Science,* 1973, *11,* 1-52.

Madaus, G., Airasian, P., & Kellaghan, T. *School effectiveness: A reassessment of the evidence.* N.Y.: McGraw-Hill, in press.

Madaus, G., & MacNamara, J. *Public examinations: A study of the Irish leaving certificate.* Dublin: Educational Research Centre, 1970.

Madaus, G., & Rippey, R. Zeroing in on the STEP writing test: What does it tell a teacher? *Journal of Educational Measurement,* 1960, *3,* 19-25.

Math a big problem for Florida schools. *The New York Times,* December 7, 1977.

McClung, M. Competency testing: Potential for discrimination. *Clearinghouse Review,* 1977, *2,* 439-448.

Messick, S. The standard problem: Meaning and values in measurement and evaluation. *American Psychologist,* 1975, *30,* 955-966.

Mills, R., & Bryan, M. *Testing . . . grouping: The new segregation in southern schools?* Atlanta, Ga.: Southern Regional Council, 1976.

Nathan, J., & Jennings, W. Educational bait-and-switch. *Phi Delta Kappan,* 1978, *59,* 621-624.

National Association of Secondary School Principals. *Competency tests and graduation requirements.* Reston, Va.: Author, 1976.

Pipho, C. *Update VIII: Minimal competency testing.* Denver, Colo.: Education Commission of the States, November, 1977.

Pipho, C. Minimum competency testing in 1978: A look at state standards. *Phi Delta Kappan,* 1978a, *59,* 585-588.

Pipho, C. *State activity minimal competence testing.* Denver, Colo.: Educational Commission of the States, May, 1978b.

Regents block tests as too easy. *The New York Times,* February 13, 1978.

Regents replacing competency tests. *The New York Times,* May 26, 1978.

Regents toughening high school exams. *The New York Times,* May 25, 1978.

Southeastern Public Education Program. *A citizen's introduction to minimum competency programs for students.* Columbia, S.C.: American Friends Service Committee, February, 1978.

Spaulding, F.T. *High school and life: The Regents inquiry into the character and costs of public education in the state of New York.* New York: McGraw-Hill, 1938.

U.S. Congress, House Subcommittee on Elementary and Secondary Vocational Education of the Committee on Education and Labor. *General issues in elementary and secondary education* (Part 1), 95th Cong., 1st sess., 1977.

Zieky, M., & Livingston, S. *Manual for setting standards on the basic skills assessment tests.* Princeton, N.J.: Educational Testing Service, 1977.

Section II: Issues and Problems

Since minimal competency testing programs are still largely untried in American education, there are many questions as to what the effects of such programs will be and what features of the programs will emerge as most problematical. In this section, we present selections which dissect the minimal competency testing movement from six different perspectives. The questions, problems, and concerns posed in the six selections discuss a host of potential issues which might impact on the minimal competency movement. It seems evident that not every issue addressed in the following chapters will emerge as a paramount concern in all programs; many of the issues will recede in importance as more experience with competency testing programs is gained, and other issues will become irrelevant in the face of particular implementation strategies adopted by different states and school districts. Nonetheless, the broad catalog of issues raised in the following selections does serve two purposes. It alerts potential implementers to a variety of problems they may face in carrying out their programs, and it identifies concerns that should be addressed and resolved *before* implementation gets too far along.

In the first selection, Airasian focuses upon four premeasurement issues which require attention prior to deciding upon the nature of the minimal competency testing program to be adopted. The four issues discussed are: (1) the likely success of efforts to legislate increases in pupil achievement; (2) instructional uncertainties; (3) the dangers inherent in the language associated with competency testing; and (4) determining who is to be accountable for student learning. Brickell's classic paper poses seven questions or key notes which should guide policy decisions: What competencies will be required?; How will competence be measured?; When will competency be measured?; How many minimums will be set?; How high will the minimums be?; Will the minimums be for students or schools?; and What will be done with the incompetent? These two selections should provide a clear indication of the conceptual complexity and diversity associated with minimal competency testing programs.

Madaus provides a brief overview of a number of technical and measurement issues associated with testing and standard setting. Among the areas discussed are standard setting, test selection, test security, and test validity. Since the focus in most minimal competency testing programs is upon certifying each individual pupil's learning, careful attention must be directed to the technical aspects of such programs. Madaus and Airasian, in the following selection, use the external examination system practiced widely in European countries as a basis for inferring the likely effects that competency testing programs in America will have upon students, teachers, and curricula.

McClung cites six potential legal issues in the area of discrimination which could result from poorly planned and implemented competency testing programs. Among the areas which McClung suggests may form the basis of legal challenges are: racial discrimination, inadequate phase-in periods, and inadequate remedial instruction.

The final selection in this section discusses cost implications of minimal competency testing programs. While it is impossible to provide precise estimates of actual dollar costs in many areas—due to the varying nature of the programs that will be implemented—this chapter lays out four general cost domains and lists particular cost categories within these domains. The cost domains are: (1) program development; (2) administration and implementation; (3) after-effects of implementation; and (4) intangibles.

At the completion of this section, the reader should have a good grasp of the problems, uncertainties, and likely consequences which are involved in minimal competency testing.

Chapter Five

Premeasurement Issues in Minimal Competency Testing Programs

Peter W. Airasian

Introduction

Concern over minimal competency testing programs generally focuses either upon specific procedural issues, such as defining desired pupil competencies, selecting suitable measurement techniques, and setting minimum performance standards, or upon the legal, ethical, and measurement consequences of these issues. That concern is primarily over these issues is not surprising, since they encompass the practical problems faced by school districts and states in trying to carry out mandated minimal competency programs.

But there is another, prior set of issues associated with minimal competency testing programs which, though generally overlooked, also warrants attention. These are premeasurement issues which logically arise before the definition of competencies or the search for tests. They are important for three reasons: (1) they set the parameters of minimal competency programs; (2) they impact heavily upon specific procedural decisions; and (3) they are at the root of measurement and legal challenges which can arise in carrying out programs. This chapter discusses four such premeasurement issues: (1) the attempt to mandate or legislate pupil achievement; (2) instructional uncertainties; (3) the language of minimal competency; and (4) the consideration given to the question, "Who is to be held accountable for learning?"

In order to sharpen the succeeding discussion, it is appropriate to note here that although over 30 states have adopted some form of minimal competency testing program, no two states' programs are identical. While state programs differ on a number of dimensions, including the purpose of the program (diagnosis, assessment, certification for high school graduation, etc.), the level at which the program is administered (state-wide versus individual districts), and the time at which testing begins, my comments are directed toward minimal competency programs which tie measured pupil competence to the receipt of a high school diploma. This form of minimal competency testing is most controversial and best illustrates the importance of the four issues I wish to discuss. It should be noted, however, that much of the following discussion is germane to other forms of minimal competency testing.

The Attempt to Mandate or Legislate Pupil Achievement

What is most interesting in the rise of the minimal competency testing movement is the fact that it represents a reaction on the part of the general public to a perceived decline in the quality of education. A primary push for minimal competency programs has tended to come from the general public, through state legislatures and state boards of education. The direct result of this pressure has been a series of legislated or mandated competency programs which tie a pupil's test performance to high school graduation and which, in the end, are intended to raise pupils' achievement levels.

We must, however, be less than sanguine about efforts to legislate or mandate programs whose aim is to improve pupil achievement. Certainly the recent history of legislated educational programs belies the notion that such programs, even when backed by substantial funds, have a demonstrable impact on the achievement level of pupils.

We may contrast policy designed to affect pupil achievement directly with policy designed to affect pupil participation in or access to educational programs and resources (Wise, 1978). The latter problem, which may be considered a problem of equal opportunity associated with the distribution of resources and opportunities, is essentially a legal or political matter. When schools discriminate on the basis of race, handicap, or gender, action by the courts or higher authorities can redress the imbalance. Goals associated with distribution or access to resources or opportunities can be promoted through legislation and litigation. However, policy designed to solve the problem of low achievement is different in kind from policy aimed at resource or opportunity distribution. In the former, emphasis is less upon *access* to a program than it is upon the expected *performance* of those who receive the program (Airasian, 1977). Recent experience has shown that there is a considerable difference between legislation aimed directly at producing desired ends (e.g., minimum wage, access by women to interscholastic sports, etc.) and legislation aimed at establishing means or programs which indirectly, in some presumed but not clearly understood way, will lead to desired ends. The problems of low achievement are technical in nature, more related to the means of education than to its ends. For example, we may legislate equal access to schools for different racial and ethnic groups, but it is quite another matter to presume that equal access will, in and of itself, produce equal achievement by the groups. The latter aim requires a much more detailed consideration of the methods and strategies of instruction.

Similarly, for minimal competency programs, questions such as 'how does one define minimal competency?,' 'can competencies be taught to all pupils with reasonable hope of success?,' and 'are suitable and effective remedial strategies available to help hard-core underachievers attain the competencies?,' must be addressed and resolved before we can hope to increase substantially pupil achievement. These are questions of means, not ends, and it seems clear that some legislatures and state boards of education have failed to recognize these as issues—or have assumed that they are easily resolved—in mandating minimal competency programs.

The goals of eradicating illiteracy and of increasing pupils' achievements are surely appropriate educational goals. Whether these goals can be attained through legislated or other mandated efforts to install minimal competency testing programs in schools or through greater consideration and support of instructional research—or in neither way—is a question to ponder. What is clear, however, is that the installation of minimal competency programs tied to high school graduation in the absence of consideration of means issues will pose problems at the implementation stage and thereafter.

Instructional Uncertainties*

Although the ultimate aim of minimal competency testing programs is to increase pupil achievement, most programs contain a series of intermediate aims which define implicitly the process through which student achievement is to be increased. Thus, people variously see minimal competency testing as a device to make students work harder, to increase emphasis on the 3R's in school, to hold teachers and administrators accountable for poor pupil performance, to increase the cost-effectiveness of education, and to provide early diagnosis and remediation for pupils who are having learning difficulties. By and large, the lure of minimal competency testing programs resides in the perceived desirability of these aims, although historically it can be demonstrated that programs with similar purposes have not been overly successful in attaining their ends.

What is missing in the clamor for these ends is reference to the process of education—how educational practice affects, or can affect, the individual pupil. In essence, minimal competency programs, particularly those which tie test performance to the receipt of a high school diploma, are intended to alter the process of education, often without a clear conceptualization of how the process works or of its capabilities and limitations. Of course, the same statement can be made with equal validity for a host of other programs which have appeared in recent years.

*This section is from *National Elementary Principal*, 1979, *58*, 2. Copyright © 1979, National Association of Elementary School Principals. Reprinted with permission of publisher.

But it must be recognized that minimal competency programs designed to certify high school graduation are unlike most other programs with which we are familiar. In most existing programs, be these state-wide assessments, Title I projects, or local district achievement testing programs, inferences about student learning are made on the basis of aggregated data, summed and averaged over a large number of pupils. The consequences associated with individual pupil performance generally are not great or severe. Minimal competency testing programs do not focus primarily on the average performance of groups of pupils, but rather on the performance of *each individual pupil.* Moreover, the consequences of poor performance may be grave for each pupil, namely retention in grade or denial of a high school diploma. Because the focus in minimal competency testing is on individual pupils, and because there are severe penalties associated with poor performance, minimal competency programs pose a number of problems.

The focus upon individual pupil certification raises two general issues. The first is that improper instruction, faulty measurement procedures, or inappropriate standards which result in injury to individual pupils may form the basis of legal challenges once the program is underway. The second issue raised by focusing decisions upon the individual pupil relates to the characteristics of competencies selected and the instructional techniques available to teach these competencies. It is in considering this second issue that we are brought face to face with concerns about educational practices and processes.

Probably the single greatest concern in selecting competencies which will be tested to certify high school graduation is the answer to the question, "Is it reasonable to expect, given sufficient time and resources, that schools can foster these competencies in all children encompassed by the program?" If students are to be held accountable for achievement of the selected competencies and if there are sanctions associated with poor performance, it is crucial that the competencies be viewed as capable of attainment by all pupils. It is unfair to hold pupils accountable for behaviors, skills, and knowledge that are, in part, or totally, beyond the school's direct power to control and influence. It may be harder for some pupils to attain the competencies than others because of motivational, intellectual, physical, or emotional handicaps. Certain pupils, manifesting more severe handicaps in these areas, may be given an exemption from the program, as has been the case in many states. However, even among the non-exempted, some pupils undoubtedly will require more time, more remediation, and more individualized instruction to attain competencies that their peers find all too easy. But if there is doubt about whether it is reasonable to expect eligible pupils to attain a competency as a result of instruction—of whatever type, duration, and time—then serious consideration must be given before that competency becomes part of a program tied to high school graduation.

For certification in minimal competency programs, it may be insufficient to argue that, "I can guarantee teaching, but not learning." A stronger case will need to be made that the competencies sought are available, at least potentially, to all students through the instructional process. Undoubtedly, there will be pupils who will not master all, or even most, of the required competencies. There does, however, have to be a strong belief—or better yet, evidence—that the competencies selected represent achievements, in the sense that schools and teachers could foster them in pupils given the correct set of circumstances. An important distinction must be kept in mind. There is a difference between the proportion of students one expects, under optimum conditions, could successfully learn the competencies and the proportion of students who actually attain measured minimal competency. Students may fail a minimal competency test for a number of reasons; despite the fact that, potentially, mastery of the competencies was available to all.

The preceding argument is important because in selecting competencies, schools implicitly go on record as assuming the major responsibility for fostering those competencies. If they cannot, it is unfair to expect pupils to manifest the behaviors and to penalize them if they don't. This argument seems simple and straightforward, but it contains an important concern. The tendency to focus on the desirability of selected competencies diverts attention from the question of whether they are amenable to instruction in the schools. In fact, not a great deal of systematic, transferable knowledge exists about the instructional process. This is particularly true for more generalized pupil behaviors, such as the ability to apply ideas to new situations, or to synthesize disparate information into a coherent whole, not to mention a wide range of social and affective behaviors.

Some have made a distinction between two kinds of pupil competencies. The first type of competencies are called 'enablers' and include school-specific skills, such as multiplication facts, spelling, punctuation rules, etc. The second type are more generalized 'competencies' and involve the application of school-specific skills and knowledge to more life-like situations, such as balancing a checkbook, computing compound interest, etc. The state of the art in instruction is such that we are considerably more confident about teaching pupils 'enablers,' basic facts, and knowledge, than we are in effecting the transfer of these skills to life situations.

While most educators would concur that basic cognitive skills and processes do fall within the domain of teachable behaviors, there is less agreement that so-called 'higher level skills,' such as the ability to apply knowledge to the solution of unfamiliar problems, the ability to recognize unstated assumptions, or the ability to formulate appropriate hypotheses based on an analysis of the factors involved in an unfamiliar situation, can be taught successfully to all pupils. The relationship of general intelligence to mastery of these more abstract behaviors belies the notion that they are readily available to all students (Madaus, Nuttall, and Woods, 1973). Moreover, and perhaps most crucially for competency testing programs, it is not at all clear how pupils acquire such behaviors or the types of instructional materials that are most appropriate for developing them. The issue here is not that these behaviors cannot be taught, but rather that teaching them, given the present state of knowledge about instruction, is as much an art as a science. Techniques useful with some pupils are not useful with others; strategies adopted by one teacher are not readily exportable to other teachers. Certainly, minimal competency

programs which seek such outcomes will face instructional
problems which involve a degree of complexity far removed from
the simple 'diagnose and prescribe' language contained in the
description of most competency-based programs (Madaus and
Airasian, 1977).

If the domains of personal, social, and career development are
to be tested as part of a minimal competency program, and if
these domains involve more than cognitive and psychomotor
competencies, then it may be particularly difficult to design
appropriate instructional techniques for the development of such
competencies. Even when the issues of whether the school *should*
teach confidence, self-concept, work ethic, or job preparedness are
put aside, serious questions remain about whether schools *can*
teach such affective competencies to all pupils. To date, programs
in these areas have not met with marked success, and the prospect
for widespread, universally successful teaching of such objectives
remains a hope rather than a reality. Educators simply do not
know a great deal about systematic approaches to effect changes
in such behaviors. An additional set of legal problems may be
associated with efforts to teach and evaluate mandated personal
and social behaviors. Note that all of the preceding concerns are
relevant not only in the context of regular school instruction, but
also in the context of efforts to remediate pupils' learning
difficulties.

Focusing upon the ends of programs rather than upon the
means available to attain these ends has particularly important
overtones in minimal competency programs. In such programs, an
understanding of the limits of the state of the art in instruction
and curriculum is critical, because by the explicit publication of
minimal competencies, schools go on record as implying that they
can, in fact, develop these competencies; schools imply that they
can foster the competencies in pupils. There is nothing wrong with
wanting each pupil who graduates from high school to manifest
competencies which will help him or her cope with life in a
complex technological society. However, given present-day knowledge about instruction, we should think carefully about translating
our desires into a system of accountability, which places the
primary onus of responsibility on the individual pupil.

The Language of Minimal Competency

A third issue which is related to and tends to exacerbate the problems already described concerns the language which surrounds the competency movement. It was noted above that the language of the competency movement tends to be ends-oriented, focusing upon the potential products of programs rather than upon the means necessary to attain these ends. An emphasis on ends or outcomes is not unexpected, since much of the rhetoric about minimal competency programs has been generated by advocates seeking to propagate their belief in the efficiency of such programs. Moreover, much of the appeal of minimal competency is a function of its stated ends rather than a consequence of any evidence of the ability of such programs to attain these ends. The language employed in discussions of minimal competency programs, unfortunately, has the potential to raise expectations about the ability of schools to make all segments of the student population literate, without the certainty that schools can actually do this.

Consider, for example, the language used by the California State Legislature when it passed a law requiring junior and senior high schools to adopt standards of proficiency in basic skills, and tied high school graduation to these standards as of 1980: ". . . pupils attending public schools in California acquire the knowledge, skills, and confidence required to function effectively in contemporary society." Such language is not unique to the California Legislature; similar themes can be found in bills of other states. At first blush, it is difficult to fault such an intent. It holds out the promise of knowledgeable, confident pupils, successfully carrying out their chosen roles in society. Few would debate the merit of such a goal.

However, if we consider more fully the words used in the intent, we shall see that there are a number of questions left unanswered by the legislature's statement. These questions are important, since receipt of a high school diploma in California will depend upon their answers. Consider the wording more closely. What, for example, is the distinction between knowledge and skills? Is knowledge a familiarity with basic facts, such as the multiplication table, rules of punctuation, etc., while skills are applications of these facts to real-life situations, such as filling out a tax form, writing a coherent business letter, etc.? And if this distinction is correct, are we confident that schools can—or should—teach such applications to all pupils? Should every pupil have to be able to fill out a tax form, compute compound interest, etc., in order to receive a high school diploma?

More to the point, however, are the questions raised by the words used in the latter portion of the statement. Can—or should—schools teach confidence? What exactly is confidence? How much confidence is too much and how much too little? Is the possibility that some pupils may fail to demonstrate the cognitive proficiencies required for obtaining a high school diploma antithetical to the goal of instilling confidence in all pupils? What of the pupil who can demonstrate cognitive competencies but lacks confidence? Should he or she be denied a diploma? And, if so, on what basis? At a more general level, the intent to instill an affective behavior, such as 'confidence,' in all pupils raises a number of legal, ethical, and political questions about the aim and function of schools in the affective domain.

Finally, what skills, knowledge, etc., are 'required' to 'function effectively' in 'contemporary society'? There is a legitimate question—and this question should be examined empirically—as to the number of American adults who presently possess the basic skills and knowledge talked about in many minimal competency programs. What then, does 'function effectively' mean? Is there a universal norm of effective functioning which can be applied to all people, regardless of occupation, geographic location, level of education, etc., to define the ability to function effectively? Moreover, in a society which is changing constantly, is it sufficient to set our goals at effective functioning in 'contemporary society'? 'Contemporary society,' by definition, will not be contemporary in five or ten years and the skills, knowledge, and confidence required to function in 1979 may be quite obsolete by 1989.

The California legislation was singled out for discussion, but the same argument could have been made using other states as examples. Had this been done, the arguments made would have been similar, but the terms may have been different (e.g., survival skills, minimal competency, life skills, functioning members of society, etc.).

If one examines the California State Legislature's intent vis-a-vis its minimal competency program, one sees that the second half of the intent, 'required to function effectively in contemporary society,' is really a justification for the first half, 'acquire the knowledge, skills, and confidence.' We have just seen that the fuzziness of this terminology and the questions it raises cloud both the intent and specifics of the legislation. It appears that there are at least two ways to justify the need for a minimal competency program. The first is to justify the program in terms of some wider societal functioning and adequacy, which is what the California legislators have done. The second is to say simply that high school graduates should have certain competencies because the community believes and wants pupils to have them, thereby avoiding statements which directly tie competence to 'survival' or 'effective functioning' in society. The way in which a legislature or state board of education chooses to justify its minimal competency program directly impacts on the type of validity a test of minimal competency must possess. The validity question, in turn, inevitably raises other legal and ethical problems.

It needs to be understood clearly that the rationale for the adoption of any minimal competency program resides in the value domain. Whether or not a state or district has a minimal competency program will not be decided on the basis of empirical evidence. Such evidence may explain or describe particular characteristics of the program, but the evidence itself will not determine the program's adoption or defeat. People will do this, and they will do it on the basis of value judgments about the worth of the program and the competencies such a program encompasses.

It is not necessary to prolong unduly this discussion about the language of competency, but it is worthwhile to point out the seductive nature of the terminology used to describe and justify minimal competency programs. Undefined, perhaps undefinable, terms are used in discussing such programs, and it is only when one thinks through the meaning and application of such terms that the apparent simplicity of minimal competency testing is stripped away, revealing its true complexity. The present language of minimal competency programs often does a grave disservice by masking this complexity and by falsely raising expectations about what programs will accomplish.

**The Consideration Given to the Question,
"Who Is to Be Held Accountable for Learning?"**

Different publics hold different educational groups responsible for students' poor achievement. Some hold students themselves to blame, others fault teachers who are ignoring "basics" to focus on creative or humanistic objectives, still others hold administrators responsible, and some simply place the blame on the "system" itself. Although different groups wish to hold different participants in the educational process accountable for student achievement, it is clear that when minimal competency testing is tied to high school graduation, the onus of accountability falls squarely on the individual pupil.

There are many reasons for this, ranging from the failure of states and locales to consider in advance of program implementation just who they wish to hold accountable, to political and logistical problems in trying to hold anyone save students accountable for their own learning. Given that much of education is sequential and cumulative and that most skills measured by minimal competency tests are learned over a number of grades, it is very difficult to hold an individual teacher accountable for the fact that at grade eight or ten, a pupil cannot demonstrate mastery of certain basic skills. While one could quite justifiably argue that the system is at fault, the only *individual* who can be held directly accountable is the pupil. So long as minimal competency programs restrict the assessment of competencies to the junior or senior high school years—after two-thirds of a pupil's time in school is completed—it will be extremely difficult to hold any individual teacher or school accountable for a pupil's performance on a minimal competency test.

It is not the purpose to argue here that students should not be held accountable for their learning. Rather, the intent has been to point out that *by default,* largely as a result of the procedures adopted in some states, the student assumes the primary onus of accountability. Since the potential consequence of failing a minimal competency test may be grave—denial of a high school diploma—and since there are many unresolved issues associated with the capability and limits of school instruction, it seems important that the question of accountability be explicitly considered before a minimal competency program is enacted.

It is important to ask, "Whom do I wish to be accountable, if anyone?" Is the concern primarily with teachers, pupils, or school curricula in general? If sanctions for student failure are to be applied in a minimal competency program, it is necessary that the reasons for applying the sanctions to a particular group be clearly thought through in advance of program implementation. We may ultimately decide that the student bears final responsibility for his or her learning, but we should decide this explicitly, considering all that has been noted previously, not let it be decided by default or by the particular way we implement a minimal competency program, as has happened in many states.

The question of accountability obviously is not a simple one. It involves the decision to hold some group or the 'system' responsible for student learning and hence has political, economic, educational, and ethical aspects. It has not been argued that any particular individual, group, or organization be singled out as the object of accountability. It has been suggested, instead, that since a minimal competency program is a form of accountability, a potentially harsh form, it is essential that the issue of who is to be accountable, and how accountability will be determined, be thought through before the program is instituted.

In thinking through the problems of accountability, it may become apparent that primary concern is with hard-core under-achievers rather than with all students who attend high school, or with a few teachers who ignore 'basics' rather than with teachers in general. Moreover, it may be recognized that competency testing at grade eight or above is inefficient for identifying pupil learning needs at a time when remediation can be most beneficial.

Consideration of such issues prior to program definition and implementation not only could alter substantially the nature of the minimal competency program initially envisioned, but also could overcome many of the potential measurement and legal concerns.

Conclusion

This discussion has tried to highlight four issues which should be addressed *before* installing minimal competency testing programs. It was suggested that these areas have not received adequate attention in many of the minimal competency programs which have been implemented to date. The problems of minimal competency testing programs are not confined exclusively to questions about testing procedures and standard setting. Rather, the spectre of minimal competency gives rise to more fundamental questions associated with the instructional capabilities and limitations of schools, the propagation of false or inflated expectations, and the appropriate locus of responsibility for pupil learning. While such questions clearly are related to the search for suitable standards and measurement techniques, they also are important in their own right and should not be overlooked.

References

Airasian, P.W. Societal experimentation. Invited address at the Annual Conference of the British Psychological Society, University of Exeter, Exeter, England, April, 1977.

Madaus, G.F., & Airasian, P.W. Issues in evaluating student outcomes in competency-based graduation programs. *Journal of Research and Development in Education,* 1977, *10,* 3, 79-91.

Madaus, G.F., Nuttall, R.L., & Woods, E. A causal model analysis of Bloom's taxonomy. *American Educational Research Journal,* 1973, *10,* 4, 253-262.

Wise, A.E. Minimum competency testing: Another case of hyper-rationalization. *Phi Delta Kappan,* 1978, *59,* 9, 596-598.

Chapter Six

Seven Key Notes on Minimal Competency Testing *

Henry M. Brickell

I want to strike not one but seven key notes, since the policy you compose for minimal competency testing must have seven themes or it will be an unfinished symphony. That is, there are seven things to think about, seven elements in your competency policy:

1. What competencies will you require?
2. How will you measure them?
3. When will you measure them?
4. How many minimums will you set?
5. How high will you set the minimums?
6. Will they be for schools or for students?
7. What will you do about the incompetent?

What Competencies?

That is the first question.

Begin by distinguishing between school skills and life skills,

---

*Reprinted with permission of the author and the Education Commission of the States.

between the skills it takes to get by in school and the skills it takes to get by in life, between those needed to succeed later in school and those needed to succeed later in life.

There is a difference. And there are different tests for them. Here is a question from a *school-skills* test:

- If John has 70 marbles and gives Joe 13 marbles and gets 26 marbles from Slim and gives 38 marbles to Alice, how many marbles does John have left?

And here is an item from a *life-skills* test:

- Balance this checkbook by adding these deposit slips and subtracting those canceled checks.

Both require arithmetic but the first one—although it sounds easier—requires the student to abstract the ideas, decide to add and subtract, and arrange the numbers before making the computation, while the second one does not. The first are classic skills of the school room, excellent predictors of success in higher levels of mathematics. In fact, it is more important to set the problem up correctly than to get the right number of marbles—if we are talking about *school skills.*

But if we are talking about *life skills,* getting the bank balance right is everything.

Here is another *school-skills* question:

- If there are 77 teeth in 2 3/4 inches of hacksaw blade, how many teeth are there in 3 1/3 inches?

Here is another *life-skills* question:

- To saw very hard metal, should you buy a hacksaw blade with few teeth or many teeth?

The first will indicate whether the student is ready for the next course in school; the second will indicate whether the student is ready for the shopping center. Both are important. Which competencies should you require?

How about school skills for the college-bound and life skills for the job-bound? Or maybe both for everybody? How about school skills for promotion to the next grade and life skills for graduation from school? Or maybe both at every point in school so that every student must climb a stepladder of learning with its rungs held up on two sides: school skills on one side, life skills on the other side?

Of course, there are basic skills—such as reading, writing, and arithmetic—used in both school and life, which is why we call them "basic." See Figure 6.1.

Thus, you have five choices. You could test competency in each:

1. Basic skills.
2. School subjects.
3. Life areas.
4. Basic skills *applied* in each school subject.
5. Basic skills *applied* in each life area.

The obvious choice is #1: Basic skills. But wait a minute. Look at the others.

- Unless you choose #2, teachers of art and music and science and social studies and foreign languages and driver education and vocational subjects will have no minimum standards.
- Unless you choose #3, teachers can teach about school and not about life.
- Unless you choose #4, students may spell a list of words correctly in English class but misspell them in their science laboratory notebooks.
- Unless you choose #5, students may learn to add and subtract but be unable to balance their checkbooks.

But you can't select them all because schools do not have time and money for that much testing. So choose very thoughtfully. You will have to live with the consequences.

How Measured?

How will you measure the competencies?

The possibilities range from testing through actual experience to testing with paper and pencil. There are some points in between:

1	2	3	4
Actual Performance Situations	Simulated Performance Situations	School Products and Performances	Paper And Pencil

Figure 6.1

Basic Skills, School Subjects, and Life Areas

BASIC SKILLS	SCHOOL SUBJECTS				LIFE AREAS				Total
	Art	Business	English	Etc.	Citizen-ship	Work	Family	Etc.	
Reading									
Writing									
Arithmetic									
Etc.									
TOTAL									

So you have four choices. You could test through:

1. *Actual performance* situations in later school or on the job. This is the ideal "testing." The student demonstrates minimal competency by entering and graduating from the next level of schooling or getting a job and keeping it. The trouble is that such "testing" is expensive; it takes years; and the results come back too late to help either the school or the student.

2. *Simulated performance* situations set up in the school-house to resemble those in later school or on the job. This is good testing. The student demonstrates minimal competency in artificial situations like the real ones to come. This is cheaper, takes less time, and gives quicker results to help school and student correct failures. But it isn't perfect: (1) the situations are not real and the results may not match actual performance later, (2) there are few good tests available, and (3) it takes more time and money than using paper and pencil.

3. *School products and performances.* These are essays, paintings, experiments, clarinet solos, brake jobs, speeches, touchdowns—things students make or do while studying in school. This is not as good as simulated performance testing because the student usually has had help, the test pressures are missing, and it is hard to score the results. But it takes less time and money than arranging special simulations.

4. *Paper-and-pencil tests* in the classroom—what we usually think of as "tests." Most of these measure a narrow bank of knowledge or skill and are far removed from actual performance situations. Thus, the results may not fore-shadow later success in school and life, where success depends on attitudes, values, personal warmth, leadership, creativity, physical strength, and other things a person cannot show with a piece of paper and a pencil. But those tests are quick and easy and cheap and available.

To summarize, as you move away from actual performance situations in life and move toward paper and pencil, testing becomes easier and cheaper, but the test results become less likely to predict later success. Thus, a student can fail on a minimal competency paper-and-pencil test but pass in the actual performance situations of real life. Remember this later when we talk about using test results to withhold diplomas.

Now, you might want to do this: use simulated performance situations to test *life skills* and use paper and pencil to test *school skills*.

Here's why: taking a paper-and-pencil test is, in fact, an actual performance situation in school. Indeed, you could call it the most important school skill of all. In that sense, paper-and-pencil tests are not artificially removed from school, but only from life. Since a student who does well on a paper-and-pencil test today should also do well in school tomorrow, you may choose to test school skills accordingly.

Remember: different kinds of tests may give you quite different results. So decide carefully.

There is another decision you have to make; will you develop your own tests or use what is available: as you move toward paper-and-pencil and as you decide to test school skills, you will find more and more tests to choose from. And vice versa. For instance, you will find many paper-and-pencil tests of solving science problems, an important school skill, but you will find few simulated performance tests of ethical behavior, an important life skill.

When Measured?

Will you measure competencies during school or at the end of school?

Do it during school if you believe:

- You want to measure competency to move up from grade to grade in school.
- Students and their parents deserve a distant early warning if there is trouble ahead.
- Administrators need to make changes any time students do not progress: changes in curriculum, course selection, faculty in-service training. Only formal competency tests

will alert administrators to unsatisfactory learning early enough to do something about it.

Do it at the end of school if you believe:

- You want to measure competency to move out of school and into the next school or into life.
- Students learn at different rates. All students deserve enough time to reach the minimum.
- Teacher-made tests and daily classroom contact will identify students who are not making progress during school. Formal competency testing is not needed.

Now, you could measure:

- *School skills during school* to decide promotion from grade to grade.
- *Life skills at the end of school* to determine graduation.

Or, you could measure both *at the end* if you feel that:

- Even the college-bound should be competent for life (many college students have already started working).
- Even the job-bound should be competent for further schooling (adults returning to school fill half the college classrooms today).

One Minimum or Many?

Will you set one minimum for all students or will you consider ability, special talents, family background, or other factors we know affect the *learning of students*? Will you set one minimum for all schools or will you consider community characteristics, faculty composition, school spending, or other factors we know affect the *quality of schools*?

Think about student ability as one example. A single standard can be too hard for a dull student yet too easy for a bright student: impossible for the dull and thus not motivating, trivial for the bright and thus not motivating, objectionable to parents and teachers of the dull, laughable to parents and teachers of the bright, and thus acceptable to none of them.

Using a graduated standard on a sliding scale according to ability will solve all those problems. And it will instantly create others. A graduated standard expects less of some students.

"Expect less, get less" is a formula most parents and teachers don't like. A graduated standard will grant a diploma to a dull but energetic student who gets 40 points on the exam and refuse a diploma to a bright but lazy student who gets 60 points on the exam. Moreover, current ability tests may not give fair and accurate measures and thus cannot guide expected achievement.

Is there a compromise with the best of both worlds? Yes, but it also has the worst of both worlds. You can use a low minimum for every student regardless of ability and a graduated minimum for students of, say, above-average ability. This does not expect the impossible from anyone but it does expect more from students who clearly can do more. The old problems—such as how to measure ability—are still there, of course.

The identical principles apply to setting single standards vs. graduated standards for schools as for students. A single standard may demand nothing of a wealthy suburban school and the impossible of a poor ghetto school. A graduated standard may label poor schools as places without hope or give them an excuse for not improving, neither of which is good for students, teachers, or administrators.

Perhaps you should set a separate standard for each student, considering his or her ability, special talents, and background—a standard negotiated among student, teacher, and parent. And perhaps the same for each school—a separate standard negotiated among board, administration, and faculty. Admittedly, the logistics would be formidable.

You may want to arrange several minimums into a graduated sequence to check student progress from grade to grade. Again, you may want to set a rough, general minimum immediately and refine it into specifics over the years ahead.

How High the Minimum?

If you take a cross-section of a school at any grade, you will find that some students are actually performing far above that grade and others far below. Some fifth graders do eighth grade work, while others do second grade work. Some twelfth graders do college work, while others do sixth grade work. The school is a staircase with one step labeled "seventh" but only half the 12-year-olds are standing on it.

Recently, a group of high school teachers made two minimal competency tests for the end of tenth grade: one in English, the other in mathematics. Any student who failed would get remediation, possibly two years of it, and possibly no diploma—good reason for the teachers to make the tests fairly easy and good reason for the students to try fairly hard.

I saw the tests and would say they were about fifth grade—long division, spell "separate," things like that—with a passing score of 60 percent. Not very hard. About 25 percent of the tenth graders flunked the English; about 50 percent flunked the math.

I talked with the teachers and principals afterward:

- "Suppose remediation doesn't work," I said. "Students haven't learned it in five years and may not in two more. Then what? How many diplomas can you withhold at commencement—as many as 20 percent?"
- "Of course not! Parents wouldn't stand for it. The Board, the administration, and the faculty would cave in under the pressure," they said.
- "Then how many diplomas can you refuse? How about five percent," I said.
- "Make that three percent," they said.
- "All right, three percent. Then 97 percent *have* to pass the minimal competency tests. What can you teachers and principals *guarantee*—not wish—that 97 percent of all graduates can do?" I said.
- "Guarantee? Really *guarantee* for 97 percent? Well, first grade work; maybe second grade—if you mean a guaranteed minimum," they said.
- "Won't that be embarrassing to the school?" I said. "Second grade work?"
- "Not as embarrassing as withholding 20 percent of the diplomas," they said.

You need to understand that, traditionally, minimums are something schools try for, not guarantee. They are goals, not standards. "Zero defects" is not a schoolhouse expression; "each student to his or her own potential" is. And just as that potential has no upper limit, it has no lower limit.

How many students can your school or state afford to remediate—or not promote or not graduate if remediation fails—afford both economically and politically? About ten percent, more or less? Certainly it isn't 20 percent, the percent failing competency tests in many places today. Say it is five percent. Whatever it is, the percent failing the test will probably be higher. If you can't raise students to meet the minimum, will you lower the minimum to meet the students? Those are the only two ways to guarantee that 95 percent will succeed.

You need to think ahead about that. Better choose a passing score, make a pilot run with your tests, see how many students fail, and decide whether to raise the students or lower the tests. A too-difficult test will embarrass you with too many failures and you will have to cut loopholes in it to let students escape—grandfather clauses, setting very low passing scores to start with and raising them year by year, and other loopholes. A too-easy test will embarrass you by being a joke to above-average students, their parents, and the taxpayers.

Don't forget the 12-year range in the achievement of "twelfth-graders." No public school in America has been able to eliminate it.

Oh, yes. There is something else about the minimum. How can you call it a "minimum" if the successful adults in town—butcher, baker, candlestick maker, doctor, lawyer, bureaucrat—cannot pass it? Should you define "successful" adulthood as being off welfare and out of prison, give the test to a cross-section of adults, and then make the passing score equal the lowest score made by any successful adult in town? In short, what do you mean by "minimally competent"? Can you find an adult example of it walking the streets and pick his or her test scores as your standard? How could you justify making it any higher?

For Schools or Students?

One state has a new set of reading tests for grades four, eight, and twelve. What should it set as the minimum score on each test? To get the answer, that state set up an independent panel of teachers, administrators, and citizens. Then it told the panel what it meant by "minimum":

- The minimal acceptable outcome is defined as the percentage of fourth graders you believe *must* be able to correctly respond to the item for you to consider reading instruction to be meeting the *minimal* needs of our students.
- In making your decision on minimal acceptable performance, you will want to consider: (1) the importance of the skill being measured by the item; and (2) the intrinsic difficulty of the item itself. If the actual student performance on the item falls below the percentage figure you select, then you would consider present instruction in that skill area to be unacceptable.

And it gave the panel an example:

- In this example, the estimate for the minimal acceptable outcome is 40 percent. If the actual outcome were below 40 percent, you would feel very concerned about instruction of the reading skill measured by the particular item.

And if more than, for example, 70 percent got the answer right, you would feel rather satisfied, the state went on to explain to the panel.

But what about the other 30 percent who got it wrong? How could the panel possibly be satisfied with the performance of that 30 percent? The answer is that the panel was not looking at the 30 percent as individual students. It was only looking at overall school performance. And if 70 percent of the students got the right answer, that was good enough. In short, that state wanted a minimum for the school, not for each individual student.

But what will you do: will you judge students or will you judge schools? Must each person measure up or must each program measure up? Can the school program succeed even though some students fail?

Can you see how important the difference is? It determines whether you will write test items all students can pass or only most students can pass; whether you will test everybody or only a sample; whether you will report results to each individual parent or only to the general public; whether you will settle for a school program that reaches, say, 70 percent of the students even if that 70 percent misses, for example, every single disadvantaged child; and whether you will modify every unsatisfactory program or fail and recycle every unsatisfactory graduate.

You can see the difference in costs, types of tests, demands on the professional staff to teach every student, pressures on each student to succeed, and political action by parents of each student who fails.

What About Incompetents?
   What will you do about incompetent *students*?
   1. Verify the findings independently before acting?
   2. Give them several more chances?
   3. Lower the standard so they can pass?
   4. Remediate so they can pass?
   5. Refuse to promote or graduate them until they can pass?
   6. Promote or graduate them with a restricted diploma or certificate of attendance?
   What will you do about incompetent *schools*?
   1. Verify the findings independently?
   2. Give them several more chances?
   3. Lower the standard so they can operate?
   4. Redesign their programs to match successful programs?
   5. Refuse to let them operate unless they meet the standard?
   6. Let them operate but refuse to accredit them?

You notice the parallels, of course. Whether you are requiring each student to be competent or each school to make a majority of its students competent, you can check the findings, give another chance to succeed, lower standards, modify the program, insist they meet standards before continuing, or let them go on but advertise their shortcomings to outsiders.

If *students*, each incompetent one must be held back, or remediated, or labeled and sent on. If *schools*, current students can be moved through uninterrupted but, to help future students, the school must be closed, or improved, or left open but have a skull and crossbones painted on the door.

Summary

There is a lot to think about in a minimal competency program: what competencies, how to measure, when to measure, one minimum or many, how high the minimum, for students or for schools, and what to do with the incompetent.

Chapter Seven

Measurement Issues in Minimal Competency Testing

George F. Madaus

There are a series of methodological problems associated with implementing a minimal competency testing program. In this chapter, a number of these issues will be highlighted. A detailed technical discussion is not the intent, but instead, the purpose of this chapter is to call attention to a number of measurement issues that need to be considered in implementing a minimal competency testing program. Specifically, six topics will be discussed: setting standards, norm- and criterion-referenced testing, the use of total versus part scores, test security, item difficulty, and test validity.

Setting Passing Standards

Historically, it is quite clear that certification examinations are taken seriously when it is evident that not everyone passes them and when there are serious rewards or sanctions associated with them. Thus, standard setting is a key element in any certification testing program. Unfortunately, the process is largely subjective and judgmental in nature. While much has been written about statistical approaches to determining the particular score that will minimize incorrect decisions, all approaches rely ultimately on subjective judgments regarding the relative loss incurred by erring in one direction as opposed to another. Comparisons of alternative statistical approaches, all technically sound, yield very different results (Glass, 1978). Thus, although at first glance it appears as if the statistical technology were available for determining cut-off scores, there is no consensus of any one approach, and all approaches rely on subjective judgments of some sort. Excellent, comprehensive, and quite readable reviews of the advantages and disadvantages of various methods of setting standards are provided in Hambleton and Eignor (1978) and in a special issue of the *Journal of Educational Measurement* devoted to the topic (1978).

Even if a statistical method for determining a passing score on a minimal competency test could be agreed upon, other problems still exist. What if the agreed-upon passing score resulted in 70 percent of all students failing the test? The score may have been set on the basis of sound technical procedure, but is it politically, economically, and educationally sound in light of the high failure rate? There are obvious costs involved in failing a high percentage of students, including monetary, political, and, of course, educational costs. Increased remedial services would be required. Increased frustration for parents and students would result. There are issues related to failing too *few* students as well. These include making the test results meaningless, failing to impact on teacher practice, and so forth. In reality, the determination of a suitable passing score on a minimal competency test is as much a political problem as it is a technical one. A larger part of what enters into determining the passing score is the answer to the question, "What percentage of students can we reasonably fail?" This question, in turn, is predicated upon a host of factors in addition to a statistical method for setting a passing score.

Whatever standard is finally decided upon, the reliability of the decisions made using that standard is a central concern (Hambleton and Novick, 1973; Huynh, 1976). Commonly used reliability indices, such as test-retest or internal consistency, will not suffice. Instead, information about the reliability of the decision—not the score—will need to be obtained, since the important consequences of testing flow from an individual's classification, not his or her test score.

The issue of standard setting is one of the most discussed and debated topics in the minimal competency movement. Suffice it to reiterate that any standard rests ultimately upon a value judgment and as such will be subject to intense scrutiny and criticism when used to make crucial decisions about individuals.

The Use of Norm- Versus Criterion-Referenced Tests

A norm-referenced test is one in which the scores are interpreted in terms of the pupil's performance relative to that of a comparison group. Norm-referenced scores generally take the form of grade equivalents, percentiles, or standard scores. Some minimal competency testing programs use a commercially available, standardized, norm-referenced exam as their test of minimal competency. The average performance of students at a particular grade level becomes the standard accepted as indicative that the student has mastered the minimal competencies. For example, in order to be certified "competent," a student might have to perform at a level equivalent to or higher than the average performance of students beginning the ninth grade. In other words, a grade equivalent score of at least 9.0 becomes the score a pupil must obtain to be certified.

There are a number of problems associated with this approach. First, the commercially available norm-referenced test *de facto* defines and selects the competencies being certified. It may be extremely difficult to find an available test that covers the skills which the district or state wishes to certify. Further, these questions inevitably arise: Why accept the average performance of a ninth grader as the criterion for a high school diploma? Why not the performance of the average 12th grader? There is, of course, a very good reason for this. A grade equivalent of 12.0 would correspond to the median score attained by entering 12th graders in the norming population. Consequently, one-half of the 12th graders fall above this point and one-half below. To set the cut-off score at 12.0, therefore, would mean that on the average only one-half of the 12th graders taking the test would be certified. The percent would be even smaller for 11th and 10th graders. Thus, a grade equivalent of 9.0 is politically more acceptable. To circumvent the problems of using a grade equivalent score as the criterion for passing a minimal competency test, it may be wise to avoid the language of grade equivalents altogether.

If a norm-referenced test can be found that encompasses the desired competencies or if a norm-referenced test is specially designed, then standard scores might be a preferable metric to use in setting passing scores. Although percentiles do not have the problems of grade equivalent scores, they could be confused by the public with percentages used in traditional grading or marking. If a norm-referenced test is used, then information about the reliability of the decisions made on the basis of the test will be important. Presently, test publishers do not provide such information in their manuals.

Now, let us turn to criterion-referenced tests, which do *not* reference a student's performance to that of a norm group. There are two meanings associated with criterion-referencing (Glass, 1978). The first is that a standard of performance is predetermined, and students meeting or exceeding that standard pass, or are classified as having mastered the competencies, whereas students who score below the predetermined cut-off score fail. The intended purpose of a criterion-referenced minimal competency test is to separate students into two groups, those who have mastered the competencies and those who have not. This type of criterion-referencing is not without its problems, however; the major problem being the one pointed out above, that is, how does one determine in advance what an appropriate standard or cut-off score should be?

The second meaning of criterion-referencing is that the test is designed and constructed in a manner that defines explicit rules linking patterns of test performance to behavioral referents (Jackson, 1970). Some people mistakenly think that a score of 80 percent on a minimal competency test gives us information about what a pupil can do in some absolute sense. This assumption is not completely correct. It is true that the percent of items answered correctly by a pupil is independent of how his or her classmates do on the test and, hence, is not norm-referenced. However, unless all the items on the test are clearly linked to a group of related competencies, the percentage score tells us nothing about what a student can or cannot do relative to the tested competencies. A score of 80 percent can be said to be criterion-referenced only in the sense that some arbitrary criterion or cut-off score has been set. It is not criterion-referenced in the second and more widely accepted sense. This point needs to be kept in mind when publicity about minimal competency tests starts to be formulated by the sponsoring agency. To date, criterion-referenced tests referenced to a skill domain have not been employed as part of minimal competency graduation programs. It is misleading to bill the competency tests as criterion-referenced unless there is a link to a clearly specified skill domain.

Interestingly, if each district is permitted to set its own certifying test and standards, then the comparability of the diplomas issued by different districts is questionable. A standard set at 70 percent of the test items answered correctly by one district on its test may not be equivalent to the 70 percent set by another district on its test. Even if the two tests measured the same competencies, the item difficulty levels could vary, thus making one test considerably harder than the other. I will return to issues of item difficulty presently. In the British system, where the certifying tests are uniform within a year but different from year to year, it is recognized that obtaining a pass or honor score in one year is easier or harder than in another. Comparability of standards between districts and over time is an important consideration that must not be overlooked or lightly dismissed.

As noted, regardless of whether one adopts a norm- or a criterion-referenced test, it is important to determine the stability of the decisions made using the test.

Total Versus Part Scores

Related to the problem of standard setting is the issue of the nature of the score used to certify the competencies. A single total test score, either across subject areas or within a single subject, may be suitable for making a pass/fail decision for certification purposes, but it is virtually useless for the purposes of diagnosis and remediation. The total test score approach allows for the possibility of a student attaining the cut-off, or criterion score, by correctly answering all items related to certain competencies, while incorrectly answering all items related to other competencies. If this happens, should that student be certified as having attained the required competencies? Further, if a test covers heterogeneous competencies, and a single cut-off score is used to determine whether a student passes or fails, then questions about the meaning attached to that score can be raised. In such a situation, a state or school district would not be certifying each competency, but instead that the pupil answered a certain percentage of heterogeneous items correctly. Such a procedure would hide more than it shows and can easily mislead the public, who might naively believe that each separate competency is being certified.

If the state or district wished to certify pupil mastery of *each* competency, then a separate test for each competency would have to be built. This would be fiscally expensive and could quickly become prohibitive in terms of the testing time required of candidates. A competency-by-competency scoring procedure also increases the record-keeping task.

An alternative would be to build a separate test for each major class of competencies (i.e., computation, reading, writing, listening, etc.). The drawback to this approach is that a pupil could pass two or three tests and fail the remainder. As in the case of the external exams used in European countries, the certifying agency might have to certify performance on each test but require that all tests be passed before a diploma was issued, again complicating record-keeping.

Separate scores for separate competencies would give more information in terms of performance. However, it should be pointed out that even if separate scores are used, their diagnostic value in terms of planning remediation programs for an individual or group is slight. A separate diagnostic test would have to be built to pinpoint specific weaknesses. The construction of diagnostic tests involves developmental costs over and above those associated with the construction of the certifying exam.

There are no clear answers to the issue of one total score versus scores for each competency. The suitable approach must stem from the purpose of the minimal competency testing program. If the purpose is simply to categorize each student into either the pass or fail group without regard to diagnosis and remediation for those who fail, and without regard to whether specific competencies were mastered, the total score approach may be defensible. If the purpose is to do more than that, the competency-by-competency testing approach is more defensible.

Issues of Test Security

One problem that must be anticipated in setting up a minimal competency testing program is that of test security. Completely secure testing programs in which the same test, or large portions of it, are used every year are fairly common. However, in minimal competency programs it may not be possible or desirable to build completely secure tests.

External testing programs tied to high school certification historically have been secure only to the point of administration. In past years, old New York State Regents exams could be purchased in bookstores throughout the State. In the British system, the exams move into the public domain once they have been administered. In fact, the tradition of past exams in external testing programs is inferred from available old exams and dictates how pupils study, what they study, and how teachers teach (Madaus and Airasian, 1977).

The situation of minimal competency tests which are linked to a high school diploma is not comparable to testing programs run by professional testing and certification agencies. In the latter case, the examinee voluntarily elects to sit for the exam. The examining body provides a service to the examinee for a fee, part of which goes to defray the test construction expenses, running the program, and reporting results to the examinee or to schools designated by the examinee. In the case of certifying boards in medicine, nursing, or other professions, the applicant is applying for licensure. The applicant pays a fee to sit for the organization's certification exams, which once again goes in part toward test development, maintenance, and program costs.

Most minimal competency testing programs are quite another matter entirely. First, pupils do not elect, but for all intents and purposes are required, to sit for the test. Second, the test is paid for out of tax funds. If a pupil fails the exam and is denied a diploma until he or she can pass it, it is quite conceivable that the applicant will want to question parts of the exam. Under the freedom of information law, the student might be able to demand to see the test. Once the taxpayers' monies are involved, it is only a matter of time before someone asks for the test's release, and the State will probably have to accede to such a request. If this analysis is correct, then measures will have to be taken to make each year's test comparable, and as far as possible, make the standard for passing comparable from year to year.

Another reason for making the tests public after use is that their availability permits the public to judge how well the tests measure the things it thinks are important and should be certified before a diploma is issued. Further, Jencks (1978) points out that teachers who do see commercial achievement tests argue that the tests don't measure things they want students to do or to know about. Some people in the testing profession cavalierly dismiss this reaction as teacher defensiveness. However, until tests are available for public scrutiny, such a charge of defensiveness cannot be intelligently countered. The same argument holds for minimal competency tests.

Another issue under test security is that of cheating. Techniques for the detection of cheating will have to be considered. Techniques to assure that the person sitting for the test is, in fact, the person to be certified would have to be developed. This would best be handled by the local education authorities. It should be noted that if local teachers are involved in administration, it would be next to impossible to keep a test completely secure over the long-term. This does not mean that groups of teachers cannot be involved yearly in test construction; in England, teachers play an essential role in developing the external exams (Brimer, Madaus, Chapman, Kellaghan, and Wood, 1978).

Issues of Test Item Difficulty

In building a minimal competency test, it becomes imperative that items are tried out beforehand to get estimates of their difficulty before the test is finalized. The reason for this is simple; as is the case with traditional norm-referenced tests, the items are the individual building blocks that eventually produce the obtained score distribution. Average item difficulty ultimately impacts upon the percentage of people who are certified. Thus, item difficulty cannot be separated from political considerations in setting the cut-off score. Glass (1978) has argued quite convincingly that the reason why 36 percent of the students in Florida failed the math portion of the minimal competency test while only eight percent failed the communication skills portion is that items on the math test were considerably harder than the items on the communication test. This interpretation is in sharp contrast to that made by Florida officials, who allocated considerable money for remediation in math on the basis of the test results. Glass further points out that someone writing items to cover a given topic can produce items that turn out too hard and others that turn out too easy for the intended audience but which on inspection appear to be equivalent. This phenomenon has also been encountered by the National Assessment of Educational Progress (Greenbaum *et al.*, 1976).

There are other reasons for pretesting items. Item analysis can reveal ambiguities in the item stems or distractors. Further, it can reveal items which are differentially difficult for different groups of pupils. If the test makers believe that the level of achievement should *not* differ between two groups (say boys and girls), they can reject items which are more difficult for one or the other of the groups. This procedure would result in a test in which members of both groups perform equally well on the average.

Issues of Test Validity

A central measurement issue in any minimal competency testing program is test validity. Without going into a detailed technical discussion of validity, certain issues concerning the validity of minimal competency tests need to be mentioned. If the minimal competency tests are used to certify that the pupil has acquired certain basic scholastic skills in areas such as computation, reading, writing, speaking, listening, etc., then the tests must be shown to be content valid. To demonstrate content validity, it is first necessary to define or specify the universe or domain of interest (i.e., computation), then describe or specify the skills and/or behaviors that are part of the domain (i.e., adding two-digit numbers that involve carrying, etc.). Once the domain is specified, content validity depends on the ability to demonstrate that the test item, in fact, represents the domain. If a test is content valid, then inferences can be made about a pupil's performance on the domain. Two facets of content validity appear in the minimal competency literature—curriculum and instructional validity (McClung, 1977).

Curriculum validity involves demonstrating that the items represent content and behaviors included in the curriculum materials used in the schools. This curricular facet of content validity is important because if the competencies are *not* explicitly reflected in the curriculum, then presumably they must be acquired through *extra*-school experiences, and therefore, it is unfair to include them as part of the high school graduation requirements. Instructional validity is a concept introduced by McClung (1977), who argues that it is not enough to demonstrate that the competencies are *common* to the various curricula; it must also be shown that an individual pupil received instruction directly related to the competencies required for certification. Such a demonstration could involve rather extensive record-keeping.

Edmonds (1977) has argued that instructional validity is closely linked to the legal concept of 'right to treatment.' The courts have recently ruled that the presence of adequate treatment is a necessary condition before a person can be involuntarily confined to a mental hospital. Using an analogous argument, the court might rule that before an agency could deny a student a high school diploma because he or she lacked some set of minimal competencies, the agency must show that the pupil—who was compelled under law to attend school until he or she reached age 16—received 'adequate' treatment. If such a decision were ever made, then demonstrating the 'instructional' validity of a certifying test would become very important.

If the competencies are worded in terms of life skills, i.e., balancing a checkbook, filling out a job application—determination of content, curriculum, and instructional validity is complicated. These life skills essentially ask the pupil to apply basic skills to new situations. As we saw, the hope is that specific school skills, such as addition, reading, etc., will transfer to more general life skills, such as balancing a checkbook or reading a prescription label. Content and curriculum validity may be quite hard to demonstrate for a test measuring life skills for two reasons. First, it may not be possible to define and delimit the domain of life skills. Second, such skills are not always common to the curricular materials used in the schools. Interest rates, checkbooks, tax forms, etc., were included in seventh and eighth grade arithmetic books in the 40's and 50's but dropped out of sight in the 60's with the advent of modern math, the exception being courses like business arithmetic, where such topics are still covered. Further, unless special courses, or blocks of time were specifically devoted to teaching the application of basic skills to life situations, it might be impossible to demonstrate instructional validity.

When the number of individuals to be certified is large, then direct measurement is often costly and time-consuming, and indirect measures are often substituted. However, when the competencies are stated in terms of life skills, which require the student to apply basic skills of literacy and numeracy to real-life situations, the construct validity of an indirect paper-and-pencil multiple-choice measure of many of these skills becomes an issue. Many 'life-skill' competencies are validly measured by the most direct means possible—situational or performance tests—to determine if the student can or cannot perform these activities. Driving a car is a good example. Even when the competencies are limited to traditional scholastic areas, such as writing or listening, the validity of using indirect multiple-choice tests to assess these skills is questionable. To frame multiple-choice items that ask a student to identify an example of poor, or incorrect, writing is no substitute for the more expensive and direct measure of asking the student to write a paragraph or a business letter. In the case of writing and listening, the relationship between such direct and indirect measures is very low, and therefore, the indirect measure should not be used. Any indirect, or surrogate, measure will have to be validated against direct performance measures before it can be used. If the relationship between the direct and indirect measures is low, then the direct measure must be employed.

So far the issue of measuring affective competencies, such as the development of confidence or interest in reading or such vague competencies as becoming a 'life-long learner,' has been avoided. At the risk of being glib, these so-called competencies should not be part of a graduation requirement. Ethical concerns apart—and these should not be dismissed lightly—relative to our sophistication in evaluating cognitive outcomes of learning, our skill at evaluating these types of competencies is minuscule.

If the competencies pupils are required to demonstrate are linked to adult functioning, then the certifying agency may be required to demonstrate that the minimal competency tests have criterion validity. That is, the agency may have to show that the minimal competency tests are actually related to 'successful adult functioning.'

If the area of employment testing is any indication, then demonstrating criterion validity could prove to be a costly and frustrating task. First, a criterion measure of adult functioning would have to be developed; questions about the validity of this criterion measure would have to be dealt with even *before* one were to study its relationship to performance on the minimal competency tests. There are any number of ways adults can compensate for some deficit, or lack of skill, and function effectively. The definition of a term like 'effectively' is not an easy matter and ultimately is a value judgment. While it has never been required, imagine the problems we would have in showing that the test for a driver's license is related to being a successful driver—whatever that involves! Another problem is that definitions of effective adult functioning can change with technological developments in the society. Old skills can become obsolete, and the need for new skills that we cannot anticipate can arise.

Problems of defining and measuring some criterion of effective adult functioning aside, long-term predictive studies show weak relationships between scholastic or school achievement measures and success in various professions. Suffice it to say that if the certifying agency decides to word its minimal competency testing program in terms of adult functioning, then the criterion validity of the certifying test could become an issue. Certifying agencies may be better off avoiding any reference to successful adult functioning when mandating minimal competency programs.

Conclusion

The potential positive and negative consequences associated with the institution of a minimal competency testing program need to be anticipated at the outset. Only then can steps be taken to maximize benefits and avoid the very real detrimental effects that can subtly but inexorably occur with the advent of an external testing program. Since the intent of minimal competency testing is to certify individuals, specific measurement issues, particularly those related to standard setting, scoring, test security, and validity need careful attention. For some of these issues, there is no easy resolution. However, they need to be addressed and resolved as far as possible before a full-blown program of minimal competency graduation testing is instituted.

References

Brimer, M.A., Madaus, G.F., Chapman, B., Kellaghan, T., & Wood, R. *Sources of difference in school achievement.* Windsor Berks, England: NFER Publishing Company, Ltd., 1978.

Edmonds, R. Developing student competency: Alternative means and attendant problems. Harvard University, 1977 (mimeo).

Glass, G.V. Standards and criteria. *Journal of Educational Measurement,* 1978, 5, 4, 237-261.

Glass, G.V. Postscript of "Standards and criteria." Paper presented at the 1977-78 Winter Conference on Measurement and Methodology of the Center for the Study of Evaluation, University of California, Los Angeles, January, 1978.

Greenbaum, W. *et al. Measuring educational progress: A study of National Assessment.* N.Y.: McGraw-Hill, 1976.

Hambleton, R.K., & Eignor, D.R. Competency test development, validation, and standard setting. Laboratory of Psychometric and Evaluative Research, Report No. 84. Amherst, Mass.: School of Education, University of Massachusetts, 1978.

Hambleton, R.K., & Novick, M.R. Toward an integration of theory and method for criterion-referenced tests. *Journal of Educational Measurement,* 1973, *10,* 159-170.

Huynh, H. Statistical consideration of mastery scores. *Psychometrika,* 1976, *41,* 65-78.

Jackson, R. *Developing criterion-referenced tests.* Princeton, N.J.: Educational Testing Service, 1970.

Jencks, C. The wrong answer for schools is: (b) Back to basics. *Washington Post,* February 19, 1978.

Journal of Educational Measurement. Special issue on standard setting. 1978, *15,* 4.

Madaus, G.F., & Airasian, P.W. Issues in evaluating student outcomes in competency-based graduation programs. *Journal of Research and Development in Education,* 1977, *10,* 3, 79-91.

McClung, M.S. Competency testing: Potential for discrimination. *Clearinghouse Review,* August, 1977, 439-443.

Chapter Eight

Issues in Evaluating Student Outcomes in Competency-Based Graduation Programs *

George F. Madaus
Peter W. Airasian

Introduction

After a little over a decade during which the emphasis in education has been upon equality, there are indications of a recent shift toward emphasis upon educational quality. This shift is most pronounced at the high school level, where controversy over test score declines, inadequate vocational preparation, and falling standards of literacy and numeracy has centered. Whether this controversy implies a real decline in standards or merely reflects the periodic pendulum swing of public scrutiny of its schools, it is clear that greater pressure is being put on high schools to focus teaching upon the three R's and the practical skills high school students will need to cope successfully in our complex technological world.

*From *Journal of Research and Development in Education,* 1977, *10,* 3, 79-91. Reprinted with permission of the publisher. Copyright © 1977 College of Education, University of Georgia.

In a growing number of cases, the response to perceived shortcomings in high school programs has involved withholding a graduation diploma from any pupil who cannot demonstrate mastery of a set of processes, knowledges, and skills deemed essential for functioning in the out-of-school world. At present, 29 states, enrolling two-thirds of the nation's school children, have initiated or begun planning to certify students on the basis of their ability to demonstrate mastery of a specific set of pre-defined activities. Such programs have various names, but generally are referred to as competency-based graduation programs. Essentially, a competency-based graduation approach involves the specification and evaluation—by an agency external to the school—of the specific behaviors a pupil must demonstrate in order to graduate from high school. While the actual behaviors required for graduation vary from state to state or district to district, in most cases, cognitive, social, and attitudinal behaviors are included. The behaviors themselves are most frequently referred to as minimal competencies, to denote that they represent the basic, fundamental capabilities a student must demonstrate in order to function in society.* Use of the term 'minimal competencies' further implies that learning will not stop after the basics have been mastered. Although some of the graduation competencies required include areas presently emphasized in high schools, others have not been directly emphasized in most school programs (e.g., complete a tax form; follow directions on a prescription label; understand common indices for comparison buying; participate as a citizen in the community, state, and nation; use leisure time productively). There are two purposes for specifying and evaluating such minimal competencies as prerequisites to high school graduation: (1) to be able to define more clearly what an individual can do after 12 years of schooling, and (2) to insure that no pupil is certified as completing high school until he or she has demonstrated his or her mastery of minimal competencies deemed essential to functioning

---

*In some cases, the behaviors are termed 'survival competencies,' a terminology which is both misleading and confusing. Taken literally, mastery of behaviors defined as essential to survival must be absolute and total, elsewise the pupil will not 'survive' in an out-of-school context. We shall avoid the use of the term 'survival competencies' in this discussion.

in society. The perception on the part of parents, legislators, and educators who support competency-based graduation plans is that the setting and evaluation of minimal competencies by an agency external to the school provides a method for society to engage in quality control of its high school learners. Indeed, a recent Gallup Poll indicated that 65 percent of the respondents agreed that pupils should pass a standard national examination in order to get a high school diploma (Gallup, 1976).

Integral to competency-based graduation programs is the determination of whether students have mastered the desired competencies. However, given the nature of the competencies and the fact that they generally include non-cognitive as well as cognitive behaviors, the type of student evaluation required is more complex than the traditional, end-of-course evaluations which characterize current student assessment. Many of the competencies are not course specific, but rather the cumulative outcome of a number of courses or school experiences, e.g., reading with comprehension. Further, the nature of evaluation is altered, insofar as certification is not teacher- or school-specific, but is conducted under the aegis of some external body at the district or state level. Although competency-based graduation programs possess an intuitive appeal because of their clearly specified outcomes, external evaluation provision, and quality control mechanisms, they do pose a number of student evaluation problems which have rarely been encountered in American education. This discussion is concerned with such problems.

Problems Associated with Competency Specification

The issue of student evaluation in a competency-based graduation program cannot be considered independently of two crucial implementation features. The first feature is the actual setting of minimal competencies, particularly in the areas of personal, social, and career development. Defining minimal cognitive competencies is not as great a problem, since schools have tended to emphasize cognitive learning and have a fairly successful track record in teaching reading and mathematics skills. However, the process of defining minimal competencies and then mandating them as necessary for graduation raises interesting moral, legal, and educational implications. For example, how far can a state or school district go in mandating particular 'social' or 'attitudinal' competencies without violating an individual's freedom of choice? Further, by making explicit the school's responsibility to foster the defined competencies, the implication is that schools are capable of teaching them. The nature of the competencies selected for emphasis, therefore, can have enormous impact upon the success instruction can have in helping pupils to attain mastery.

A second feature, one which ultimately can have the greatest influence on student outcomes, concerns the consequences associated with failure to attain the mandated level of competence required for graduation. It is highly probable that the extent to which graduation competencies are stressed in instruction and evaluated with rigor is a direct function of how seriously the competencies are viewed as determining pupil graduation. Whether or not demonstrated competency is viewed as crucial in the teaching-learning process will depend, in turn, upon such issues as who defines and evaluates competence, how mastery is defined, the value of a high school diploma in the society, and the number of pupils denied diplomas. It is in this perspective that the problem of student outcomes must be considered.

The most prevalent danger of any competency or objective-based certification system, of which competency-based graduation programs are but one example, is the tendency to focus upon the starting and ending points of instruction with insufficient concern for the process of education. In recent years, we have seen a variety of programs akin to competency-based graduation (e.g., performance contracting, competency-based teacher education, etc.) seduced by the rationality implied in an ends-oriented approach to education, an approach which begins with clear specification of the student outcomes sought in the form of behavioral objectives or competencies. Once the ends have been operationally defined, focus typically shifts to methods of evaluating whether students have attained the ends. Too often, the instructional activities which are at the heart of the educative process, both in terms of time devoted and importance, are taken for granted. It is assumed that the state of the art is such that we are able to teach most youngsters whatever we wish to teach.

While most educators would agree that basic cognitive skills and processes do fall within the domain of teachable behaviors, there appears to be less certainty that such "higher level skills" as analysis, synthesis, and evaluation are capable of being successfully taught to all pupils. Certainly, the relationship of general intelligence to mastery of these higher level behaviors belies the notion that they are readily available to all students (Madaus, Woods, and Nuttall, 1973).

While focus upon ends rather than means has occurred in the planning and conduct of other, similar programs, it has particularly important overtones in competency programs. In such programs, not misconstruing the state of the art in instruction and curriculum is critical, because through the explicit statement and publication of minimal competencies in the cognitive, social, and career domains, schools have gone on record as implying that they can, in fact, *teach* these competencies. Schools have made themselves primarily responsible for success—and failure—by implying that they can foster a wide range of competencies in all pupils, divorced in large measure from home, parents, or church. While there is no doubt that it would be beneficial for all pupils to manifest the competencies which will help them cope with life in a complex technological society, there is a legitimate question as to whether schools can and should assume primacy in the development of all such competencies. In the end, however, failure to manifest minimal competence at the conclusion of high school is laid at the feet of the pupils. Regardless of whether appropriate instructional techniques are available to, say, foster a positive self-concept, it is the student who shoulders the blame and stigma for failure upon leaving school. In essence, if affective and some higher level cognitive competencies are strongly emphasized as graduation criteria, false expectations for the outcomes of schooling and competence of pupils may be set up, expectations not justified in the light of our actual knowledge of the teaching-learning process.* If schools are to adopt primary responsibility for a wide range of social, personal, or higher level cognitive behaviors, it would seem reasonable that we be fairly confident that such behaviors can be taught to all pupils, not just to the brightest or most able who may demonstrate the behaviors in spite of rather than because of schooling. If we are to evaluate and certify pupils on the basis of school-related learning, we must do our best not to confound our evaluations with general intelligence, home background, and other extra-school factors, lest we penalize pupils, not for their failure to achieve, but for their failure to be bright or come from the right type of home.

Effect of Pupil Evaluation in Competency-Based Programs

The effects of implementing a new student evaluation model at the secondary school level are diverse, potentially influencing not only pupils, but also teachers and the teaching-learning process itself. It is in this wider context that the evaluation issues of new competency-based graduation programs must be considered. Too often, the introduction of a new program or evaluation system leads to a focus on practical measurement problems: what instruments will be used to gather evidence about this behavior, how can we appraise pupil affect, what are the proper means to diagnose pupils' learning during instruction, and so forth. While these problems are important, concentrating on them tends to direct attention from more basic issues associated with the potential effects that student evaluation will have upon the educational process. We may consider an analogy between the geodesic dome and the teaching-learning-evaluation process. When force impinges on any point of the dome's surface, all components of the structure react to the force; the influence is felt throughout.

---

*It should also be noted that failure to consider adequately the state of the art in instruction can lead to incompatibilities among the various competencies sought. For example, what is the effect on a pupil's self-concept if he or she fails a 'minimal competency' test which he or she observes most of his or her fellow students passing?

Analogously, when change is made in one aspect of the instructional process, there is a strong potential for change in other aspects. It is within the context of such structural changes that the effects of student evaluation in competency-based graduation programs must initially be viewed. These are the real effects of a new form of student evaluation.

The specification of graduation competencies has the potential to reorient the aims and emphases of secondary education, but, it should be explicitly noted, the degree to which the educational system is 'altered' is a direct function of the degree to which teachers, students, and parents perceive the competencies as real obstacles to certification.

Ultimately, the impact of any competency-based graduation program will be dependent upon the evaluation techniques utilized to provide data about student competence and the sanctions associated with failure to demonstrate competence. If the minimal competencies are to be perceived as an integral aspect of the high school curriculum, skills to be consciously acquired and valued, the evaluation of competencies must possess two characteristics: it must be rigorous and it must involve penalties for nonmastery. The fastest way to subvert the meaningfulness of the desired competencies is for a state, district, or other evaluating agency to establish meaningless or watered down evaluation procedures, ones which assure that all pupils are certified as demonstrating mastery of the competencies. If, from the outset, most or all pupils are certified in a haphazard or unrigorous manner as having attained competence, there will be little in the way of institutional change or change in the behavior patterns of teachers and pupils. Further, the educational process variables and press of the school will not be affected in any substantial way. Perhaps a remedial program might be initiated to accommodate the few unfortunate enough to fail to demonstrate minimal competence, but few institutional changes will occur.*

*A good, non-school example of the impact that an external, certifying examination can have upon individuals' behavior is provided by the driver certification process in most states. The fact that there is a significant

The most efficient method to alter the instructional emphasis in a school or group of schools is to alter the content or form of important school examinations. Certainly, this has been the tack adopted in European external examination systems (Hotyat, 1958; Madaus, Airasian, and Kellaghan, 1971; Madaus and MacNamara, 1970). The crucial ingredient in bringing about instructional change via examination change is that the examinations being altered have some import for pupils and teachers. If the results of an examination do not influence pupil or teacher certification, job placement, college admission, and the like, there is little incentive to change practice in the light of examination changes, since examination performance carries little or no weight in affecting pupils' future plans or aspirations.

America has not had a lengthy history of state or nationally administered school-leaving examinations, although some examples, such as the New York State Regents exams, have existed. The institution of district or state-wide competency requirements for graduation necessitates movement in the direction of such external, certifying examinations. In this sense, evaluation in competency-based graduation programs represents a hybrid of the European external examination system and the traditional American certification process. In the external examination system widely practiced in Europe, an agency *external* to the school (i.e., the Regents, State Department of Education, Ministry of Education, etc.) sets a series of examinations geared to an approved syllabus of instruction. Students must pass a certain number of these examinations in order to be certified as having successfully completed a given level of education. The examinations are also used to select candidates for admission to third level education, civil service, and other careers (Madaus and MacNamara, 1970). In the traditional American certification system, on the other hand, graduation has traditionally called for the accumulation of a given number of Carnegie credits, or course credits, without the external certifying examination. New competency-based graduation re-

---

first-time failure rate leads people to take the examination seriously and to spend substantial amounts of time in preparation.

quirements suggest the need to combine these two certification processes.

However, Bloom (1969) has pointed out that *examinations which are used to make important decisions at major disjunctions in the educational system have great effects.* Similarly, Tyler (1963) states that *society conspires to treat marks in certifying examinations as the major end of secondary schooling, rather than as a useful but not infallible indicator of student achievement.* The potential impact a certifying examination can have on the educational process is great.

The specification and evaluation of graduation competencies obviously can lead to broadening the school curriculum to include skills and competencies previously neglected or treated only informally. Similarly, there is the potential to alert students and teachers to the specific competencies valued for graduation and thereby to focus teaching and learning upon these competencies. There is the likelihood that the general public, including parents and employers, will be better aware of the pupil competencies implied by a high school diploma. These and a series of other outcomes are all potentially available as a result of the addition of competency certification as a requisite for high school graduation. Undoubtedly, these reasons represent a large part of the justification for such programs.

These potential advantages should not divert attention from some potential disadvantages. If too great an emphasis is placed on the mastery of graduation competencies, a number of detrimental outcomes can also ensue. Teaching and learning can become narrower, focusing upon competencies to be evaluated, to the point of cramming or neglecting important outcomes not covered in the minimal competencies. The importance of course credits and content can thereby diminish in the eyes of teachers, pupils, and parents. Rigor in course certification may disappear or become irrelevant as courses are perceived as less and less powerful for obtaining a high school diploma. Teaching and learning can become mechanized and less spontaneous, devoted to preparing for the competency evaluation rather than educating pupils in the more general sense of the word. Most importantly, schools within schools may begin to emerge, with pupils grouped in terms of whether they represent the mass of students likely to be certified as possessing minimal competence or whether they represent those for whom attainment of minimal competence is predicted to be a problem. It should be noted that the consequences associated with competency-based graduation programs will in large measure be determined by what Europeans call 'the tradition of past examinations.' It is the history of previous examinations, their emphasis and import, which determines the instructional practices schools adopt.

In sum, the maxim that teachers and pupils prepare for the examinations and evaluations that have the most import is particularly apt in a context where certification standards and content are determined by an agency external to the school. Too little emphasis on the defined competencies can lead to few changes in instruction. Too much emphasis on the competencies and their evaluation can subvert traditional classroom instruction and replace it with a narrowly focused 'teach for the competency evaluation' orientation.

Of course, if the minimal competencies defined for graduation represent what schooling is currently perceived to be all about, there is no necessary tension between the certifying examination and classroom instruction. The experience at the University of Chicago during Hutchins' tenure as Chancellor is a classic illustration of the beneficial aspects of certifying examinations on teacher practice (Bloom, 1950). Teachers decided upon the important objectives in their courses and communicated these to the University Examiner, who constructed valid course examinations. Since teachers had initial input into the examination specifications, they did not end up coaching pupils for the examination but rather taught the topics they initially decided upon. Since the examinations reflected the teachers' instructional aims, the need to prepare pupils exclusively for certifying examinations did not interfere with the teachers' planned classroom emphases.

However, there are two factors which likely will lead to competition between the minimal competencies required for graduation and the current emphases of classroom teachers. First, the competencies generally include a number of skills, learning, practices, and attitudes not explicitly emphasized in most school courses. There will, of necessity, have to be some give and take between current aims and the competency requirements. Second, there is the very real concern that the minimal competencies can become the maximums, that students and teachers will stop trying once the minimal competencies are attained (Shepard, 1976). If the examination which certifies a pupil as having reached the level of performance required of a high school graduate is particularly powerful, in terms of its perceived importance and sanctions, this second possibility can become reality. Schools will need to walk a rather narrow line with regard to the addition of minimal competencies as criteria for graduation, a line which will clearly establish their importance for graduation but do so without doing great violence to already established teaching-learning contexts, aims, and practices. The following four sections* treat in more detail the specific effects external-type examinations can have on various aspects and individuals involved in the educational process.

1. Effects on the Curriculum

Classroom objectives and the content of external, certifying examinations can be viewed as competing for the attention and time of teachers and students. When there is a choice between emphasizing tested or non-tested objectives, it is a general experience that the objectives actually tested assume primacy. Faced with a choice between one set of objectives which is explicit in the course outline and a different set which is explicit in the certifying examinations, students and teachers generally choose to focus upon the latter. This finding holds true over

*These sections draw from "Public Examinations and the School," Chapter 15 in Madaus and MacNamara, *Public examinations: A study of the Irish Leaving Certificate.* Dublin: St. Patrick's College and Educational Research Centre, 1970; and Airasian, P.W., Kellaghan, T., & Madaus, G.F. "Previous investigations relevant to the proposed experimental design of a societal experiment on the consequences of introducing standardized tests to the Irish educational system," St. Patrick's College, Dublin, Nov. 30 - Dec. 2, 1971.

different countries and over many decades (Madaus and Mac-Namara, 1970; Morris, circa 1969; *Norwood Report*, 1943; Spaulding, 1938. Also see Bloom, 1961; Davies, 1965; Hotyat, 1958; Koerner, 1968; Mukerji, 1966; Srinivasan, 1971; and Tyler, 1963). Most studies have found that the proportion of instructional time spent on various objectives was seldom higher than the predicted likelihood of their occurrence on the external examination. Competency-based graduation programs have the potential for such dysfunction, since the Carnegie credit courses may be emphasizing different skills than the competency component of the graduation requirements. Thus, teachers who see the competency requirements as a major obstacle (and it appears that such may be the case, since the evaluation procedures for the minimal competencies will likely be new and unknown, at least in the early years of the program) could begin to concentrate upon these competencies to the detriment of work in regular courses. This danger could, of course, be minimized by a close correspondence between the Carnegie course objectives and the competency requirements.

2. Nature of the Certifying Measure

One way in which certifying examinations have come to control the curriculum is through their heavy emphasis on recall of factual materials (Crossland and Amos, 1961; Madaus and MacNamara, 1970; Morris, circa 1969; Srinivasan, 1971). In competency-based programs, insistence on recall of facts would be most likely to occur in the area of minimal cognitive competencies, although care must be taken to avoid reducing higher level cognitive and affective behaviors to the level of recall by prompting, testing only the examples given in class, and so forth. Recall is a legitimate objective. However, it can have detrimental consequences if it occupies the principal instructional emphasis. In the rush to implement competency-based programs, the temptation is to focus evaluation efforts upon recall behaviors, since these are the easiest to test and certify. To some extent, this tendency is implied by the programs' insistence upon classifying social, personal, and career development competencies as 'skills.' Performance objectives involving basic literacy and numeracy skills and higher level applications may be ignored in the teaching-learning process, if the certifying examination principally focuses on recall (Bloom, 1961; Gayen *et al.,* 1961; Morris, circa 1969; Srinivasan, 1971). In building certification instruments, this is one area that needs considerable attention.

Many of the minimal cognitive competencies for graduation will involve application of basic literacy and numeracy skills to real-life situations. Examples of such skills are the ability to fill out a job or loan application form correctly; complete a tax form; balance a checkbook; read the local newspaper with comprehension; write a business letter correctly; spell and apply the rules of grammar in written work; check on the accuracy of bills, sales slips, etc.; understand basic contracts for car loans, house mortgages, etc.; follow directions correctly on prescription labels, in cook books, etc.; understand the terms of warranties; use the public library and the town and state offices; and plan and prepare nourishing meals. These competencies are most validly measured by the most direct means possible, situational or performance examinations which determine if the student can actually perform these behaviors. Driver's license examinations again provide a good example. When the number of individuals to be tested is large, direct measurement is often costly and time-consuming so that indirect measurement is substituted. This is most clearly illustrated by indirect attempts to measure writing skills through the use of objective tests (Foley, 1971; Madaus and Rippey, 1966) and by the statements in some competency-based graduation programs which claim that evaluation will be accomplished by means of objective, multiple-choice testing. However, indirect paper-and-pencil tests measuring knowledge about the competency areas are not enough. Any indirect, or surrogate measurement must be validated against direct performance measures. The basic problem of validating indirect surrogate measures against direct measures is dealt with in detail in Furst (1958), Smith and Tyler (1942), and Foley (1971). If the competencies are important, it is crucial to establish that students can perform them. Knowing that a pupil understands the theory or components of a competency is *not* the same as knowing that he or she can actually *perform* it, unless some prior research has established this fact.

Yet, the direct versus indirect measurement problem is by no means limited to basic literacy or numeracy skills; in fact, it is more acute in the affective area. For example, a common competency that might be considered crucial for mastery in the area of becoming a "life-long learner" is that a pupil develop an interest in reading. Yet, relative to our sophistication in evaluating cognitive outcomes of learning, our skill at evaluating this type of competency is small.

Indirect methods, such as using a questionnaire to assess behavior, are sufficient if one is interested in group performance data, and the anonymity of respondents can be assured. However, once such indirect techniques are used to measure affective outcomes in order to certify *individual* pupils, one can readily predict that students will "learn" to check the expected or acceptable answers or that the individual items will be challenged as to their reliability for major certification decisions. The relationship between such indirect measures and a direct, performance measure of these outcomes could drop to zero.

To complicate matters, most competency-based graduation programs suggest that testing time will be minimal. Given the scope and complexity of most programs, this seems to us an unrealistic premise. Many of the exercises developed to certify competence in one year will not be able to be re-used in succeeding years, if cramming is to be avoided. New exercises evaluating mastery of some of the basic competencies will need to be developed frequently, if the certifying examination is to be taken seriously. This is not an impossible task, but it is time-consuming and expensive. There will be a need for a trained staff to construct appropriate competency measures. Given the potential importance of the decisions to be made on the basis of the examination exercises, one wonders how much a district or a state can rely upon non-experts to construct criterion measures. Certainly, reliance upon non-experts increases the potential for court cases related to the validity and reliability of the competency criteria.

This discussion about direct and indirect measurement and about the potential emphasis on recall of facts in external examinations is related to a more general problem associated with a performance-based approach to education: the tendency to focus upon those aspects that readily lend themselves to operational definition and measurement to the exclusion of other, less tangible, but important aspects of schooling. It is tempting to equate the more measurable aspects of instruction with what education is about. Holmes (1911) long ago recognized this danger.

> Whenever the outward standard of reality (examination results) has established itself at the expense of the inward, the ease with which worth (or what passes for such) can be measured is ever tending to become in itself the chief, if not sole, measure of worth. And in proportion, as we tend to value the results of education for their measurableness, so we tend to undervalue and at last to ignore those results which are too intrinsically valuable to be measured (p. 128).

Holmes' arguments are similar to the objections of present-day directors of compensatory programs who have argued that it is not fair to evaluate their programs with standardized achievement tests because the goals of their programs are not reflected by such instruments.

The emphasis on judging school results on the basis of appearance, on the basis of their observable, visible, measurable features, has been a feature of the 'technological' world view of the 19th century, the 'scientific' world view of the 1920's and 1930's, and the 'systems development' view of the 1960's and 1970's. There have always been those with a more individual-oriented world view who have argued that the values undergirding the wide use of tests and examinations are antithetical to good education and to the belief system of teachers (e.g., Atkin, 1968; Eisner, 1967). However, while this view of the world in general, and of education in particular, is perhaps more compassionate and sympathetic, the former, more mechanistic world view has generally predominated.

It is hard to argue against measuring 'competency,' particularly if competency implies such associated values as efficient use of public monies, maintaining standards, and good teaching. However, these benefits of testing and evaluation should not be attained at the expense of other important educational aims. Competency-based evaluations can have a beneficial impact, but only if they keep all goals of the school in sight. In light of these many issues—direct versus indirect measurement, individual versus group certification, recall of facts versus other knowledge and behavior—it seems clear that the nature of the certifying evaluation to which students will be exposed can have powerful implications for the conduct and impact of competency-based graduation projects.

3. The Effects of Certifying Examinations on Teacher Practices

The principal, negative effect of external certifying examinations on teacher practices is that much of the teaching can be devoted to coaching or cramming for the certifying tests. There are tremendous social pressures on teachers to see to it that their students acquit themselves well on the certifying examinations (Bloom, 1961; Cambridge Conference on School Mathematics, 1963; Koerner, 1968; Smith and Tyler, 1942; Tyler, 1963). Clearly, one hidden agenda in the competency-based approach is teacher accountability. To the extent teachers are held directly or indirectly accountable for student performance on the certifying measures, the areas tapped by these measures will be emphasized in teaching.

The data that will become available through competency programs have many further ramifications for accountability. Historically, it is clear that data on student competence have been employed in judging both teacher and administrator "effectiveness." As early as the 1840's, when written examinations geared to very specific cognitive competencies in English and mathematics were introduced into the Boston Public Schools by Horace Mann, the hidden agenda was to judge the relative effectiveness of the headmasters of the various secondary schools (Reidy and Madaus, in preparation). Further data on the 'payment by results' era in England, Ireland, Jamaica, and Australia also show that student achievement was directly related to teacher evaluation and salaries (Airasian, Kellaghan, and Madaus, 1972). While taxpayers have a legitimate right to accountability information, one must remember that the "threat" of such information may prompt teachers and administrators to focus on the measured competencies to the detriment of other educational achievements.

Thus, the certifying examination is clearly a two-edged sword. On the positive side, well-defined and valid performance measures can become powerful forces for re-directing teaching to better cover neglected areas and competencies. Vital curricular changes are often brought to fruition by altering the certifying examination to reflect the new objectives (Bloom, 1950; Commission on Mathematics, 1959; cf. Morris, circa 1969). The negative side of external examinations is that areas of the curriculum not directly examined for certification may be de-emphasized. In fact, if the external examination is a powerful determiner of future educational or life chances, teachers may be doing pupils a disservice by emphasizing new or non-examined objectives or competencies. Innovative teaching or the teaching of objectives not tapped by the certifying examination may actually hamper pupils' life chances by taking time and emphasis away from the objectives society utilizes to appraise competence. After a period of years, many teachers become skilled in coaching pupils for the certifying measures and resist changes in the system whose rules for success they have mastered. This danger is highlighted by Srinivasan (1971), who explored the student perceptions of what Indian teachers, working under a powerful examination system, emphasized in their classes. Srinivasan found almost a one-to-one correspondence between the teaching emphasis accorded particular topics and objectives and the weight these topics and objectives received on an external, certifying examination.

4. Effects of Certifying Examinations on Students

Certifying examinations, regardless of their faults and limitations, are facts of life. Whether the methods used to cope with such examinations are harmful to students depends, of course, on the nature of the examination system. Unfortunately, there appear to be many more reports of harmful effects than beneficial ones. Several investigators have found that students, who are under considerable pressures and anxieties, spend most of their time cramming for and worrying about certifying examinations (Bloom, 1961; Koerner, 1968; Madaus and MacNamara, 1970; Srinivasan, 1971). The certifying examinations tend to become the tail that wags the dog.

Competency graduation plans must take cognizance of such possible negative effects, although focus upon minimal graduation competencies may negate such effects, since we may expect that most students would have achieved these competencies by the end of grade 12. However, the focus upon minimal competencies raises additional issues that eventually impact on student outcomes.

By focusing on "minimal graduation competencies," the certifying mechanism may very well put most pressure on a subpopulation of the school that might be characterized as "slow learners." If this is true, one would expect that the new certification process would have little impact on the average or above average students, but might create new ways of dealing with the below average students. This, like other aspects of the program, can be a double-edged sword. It may provide needed structures that will help these students attain the minimal competency the community feels that they need. At the same time, it may stigmatize these students by singling them out for preparation to meet criteria that their peers find all too simple.* This analysis, however, is complicated by the fact that in most plans the minimal competencies go beyond basic literacy and numeracy skills, and include personal development, social responsibility, and career development skills. How often could the situation arise where a straight A, accelerated student does not have an "adequate self-concept," or

---

*Further, in the not too distant future, it will be widely recognized that the competencies a pupil manifests at the end of grade 12 are dependent upon more than the three or four years he or she spends in high school. Recognition of the cumulative nature of schooling will lead to junior high school graduation competencies and, inevitably, to grammar school graduation competencies, thereby compounding the problems noted in this chapter.

perhaps lacks "well-developed career skills," or does not have a "healthy mind or body"? Will these students be denied graduation certification? Will they somehow be singled out for group remedial aid, or will some 'individual prescription' be designed to help the students overcome these 'deficits'? Do we, in fact, have prescriptions that can help students "over-come" some of these personal or social "shortcomings"? Should a pupil at age 17 be expected to have well-developed career skills, self-concept, etc.? Can lack of certification on some competencies actually reduce proficiency on other desired competencies? If we assume that an individual's affective competencies can and should be measured (both rather questionable assumptions), how many of the minimal competencies must a person demonstrate to be certified? Fifteen out of 20, 20 out of 20?

A further feature of most plans is the public disclosure of those competencies which have been achieved. Public disclosure raises the interesting issue of the right of an individual to privacy. The requirement that performance relative to a list of competencies be summarized and displayed as part of the certifying process could lead to interesting legal questions concerning individual privacy. If an employer requires a high school transcript for employment, how much information on minimal competencies can the school district release? How long after graduation should statements about performance relative to minimal competencies be used? The presence or absence of particular affective competencies at age 17 or 18 can change dramatically after leaving school. Issues related to public disclosure of individual competencies need careful scrutiny. Even the certifying process itself involves interesting questions concerning the rights of individuals. Questions of appeal and the feasibility of providing alternative ways of demonstrating competencies need to be considered. Questions as to the right of the school to attempt to certify certain affective areas could easily be challenged by pupils and parents in the courts.

Summary

We have devoted considerable attention to the broader issues associated with implementation and evaluation of competency-based graduation plans because we feel that these issues will not only determine the success of such plans but also will have maximal impact upon students. We have endeavored to point out a wide range of potential student and school outcomes which go beyond the outcomes included in the defined graduation competencies. The issues of import are not measurement problems, but problems of goals, objectives, and values.

To review, four caveats were discussed. First, given the lack of instructional research clearly indicating the appropriate methods of teaching attitudinal and value oriented competencies, it would appear better, initially, to focus attention upon basic literacy and numeracy competencies while gathering evidence about the potential of explicitly including affective, personal, social, and career development competencies among evaluated performances. These latter areas require a great deal more thought and attention to insure fair, rigorous certification of pupil competency. Second, standards of certification must be clearly articulated. The relationship between the agreed-upon graduation competencies and course credit criteria needs to be thought through. The import of mastery of some, but not all, competencies, vis-a-vis certification must be determined and made public. Under what circumstances—if at all—can a pupil be certified despite mastery of only 80 percent of the so-called 'minimal competencies'? Third, the projection that a competency-based program will not require substantial amounts of testing or evaluation time seems erroneous. If diagnosis, prescription, and certification are to be viable, meaningful processes, much time will, of necessity, need to be devoted to evaluation. Certainly, if direct measures of social, personal, and career development competencies are to be obtained, evaluation will be a complex, time-consuming activity. To the extent that evaluation is not rigorous and complete, the importance of the competencies in their full meaning will be diminished. Finally, the individual student, and his or her competence, feelings, and life chances, assume the focal point in such plans. While there is much to benefit the pupil in terms of learning and acquiring important competencies, there are many potentially damaging pitfalls, such as labeling, stigmatizing, and engendering false or inflated expectations, which can negate the beneficial aspects of the plan. The implications of the plan for diminished student self-concept, reduced job or life opportunities, and the like must be carefully considered, particularly in light of the instructional and evaluation limitations specified in the body of this chapter. We are in a climate which tends to accept all too readily over-simplified solutions to complex problems. To attain maximum benefit from competency-based approaches, we must avoid demeaning them to the simple or atheoretic, especially when the true answers are complex and value-laden.

References

Airasian, P.W., Kellaghan, T., & Madaus, G.F. Previous investigations relevant to the proposed experiment. Prepared for a conference on The Design of a Societal Experiment on the Consequences of Introducing Standardized Tests to the Irish Educational System. St. Patrick's College, Dublin, 1971.

Airasian, P.W., Kellaghan, T., & Madaus, G.F. Payment by results: An analysis of 19th century performance contracts. Paper presented at Annual Meeting of National Council on Measurement and Education, Chicago, Illinois, 1972.

Atkin, J.M. Behavioral objectives in curriculum design: A cautionary note. *The Science Teacher,* 1968, *35,* 5, 27-30.

Baldwin, T. Industrial education. In Bloom, B.S., Hastings, J.T., & Madaus, G.F., *Handbook on formative and summative evaluation of student learning.* New York: McGraw-Hill, 1971.

Bloom, B.S. Examining. In *The idea and practice of general education.* Chicago: University of Chicago Press, 1950.

Bloom, B.S. *Evaluation in higher education: A report of the seminars on examination reform organized by the University Grants Commission under the leadership of Dr. Benjamin S. Bloom.* New Delhi, University Grants Commission, 1961.

Bloom, B.S. Theoretical issues in evaluation. In Tyler, R.W. (Ed.), *Educational evaluation: New roles, new means. The Sixty-*

eighth Yearbook of the National Society for the Study of Evaluation, Part III. Chicago: University of Chicago Press, 1969.

Cambridge Conference on School Mathematics. *Goals for school mathematics: The Report of the Cambridge Conference on School Mathematics.* Boston: Houghton Mifflin, 1963.

Commission on Mathematics. *Program for college preparatory mathematics: Report of the Commission on Mathematics.* U.S.A. College Entrance Examination Board, 1959.

Crossland, R.W., & Amos, R. What do 'O' level examinations in biology test? *Biology and Human Affairs,* 1961, *26,* 34-41.

Davies, H. *The changing grammar school.* Nottingham Institute of Education, 1965.

Davies, H. *Culture and the grammar school.* London: Kegan Paul, 1965.

Eisner, E.W. Educational objectives: Help or hindrance? *School Review,* 1967, *75,* 250-266.

Foley, J.J. Evaluation of learning in writing. In Bloom, B.S., Hastings, J.T., & Madaus, G.F. *Handbook on formative and summative evaluation of student learning.* New York: McGraw-Hill, 1971.

Furst, E.J. *Constructing evaluation instruments.* New York: Longmans, Green, & Co., 1958.

Gallup, G.H. Eighth Annual Gallup Poll of the public's attitude toward the public schools. *Phi Delta Kappan,* 1976, *58,* 2, 187-200.

Gayen, A.K., Nanda, P.D., Mathur, R.K., Duarti, P., Dubey, S.D., & Bhattacharyya, N. *Measurement of achievement in mathematics: A statistical study of effectiveness of board and university examinations in India.* Report I, New Delhi: Ministry of Education, 1961.

Holmes, E.G.A. *What is and what might be: A study of education in general and elementary in particular.* London: Constable & Co., 1911.

Hotyat, F. Evaluation in education. In UNESCO, *Report on an International meeting of experts held at the UNESCO Institute for Education.* Hamburg: UNESCO, 1958.

Koerner, J.D. *Reform in education: England and the United States.* New York: Delacorte Press, 1968.

Madaus, G.F., Airasian, P.W., & Kellaghan, T. The effects of standardized testing. *Irish Journal of Education,* 1971, *2,* 70-85.

Madaus, G.F., & MacNamara, J. *Public examinations: A study of the Irish Leaving Certificate.* Dublin: Educational Research Centre, St. Patrick's College, 1970.

Madaus, G.F., & Rippey, R.M. Zeroing in on the STEP writing test: What does it tell a teacher? *Journal of Educational Measurement,* 1966, *3,* 1.

Madaus, G.F., Woods, E.M., & Nuttall, R.L. A causal model analysis of Bloom's taxonomy. *American Educational Research Journal,* 1973, 10, 253-262.

Morris, G.C. Educational objectives of higher secondary school science. Unpublished Ph.D. thesis. University of Sydney, circa 1969.

Mukerji, S.N. *History of education in India: Modern period.* Baroda: Acharya Book Depot, 1966.

Norwood Report. Curriculum and examinations in secondary schools. London: H.M. Stationery Office, 1943.

Reidy, E., & Madaus, G.F. The uses of examinations: Horace Mann. In preparation.

Shepard, L.A. Setting standards and living with them. Paper presented at the annual meeting of the National Council on Measurement in Education. San Francisco, April, 1976.

Smith, E.R., & Tyler, R.W. *Appraising and recording student progress.* New York: Harper, 1942.

Spaulding, F.T. *High school and life: The Regents' inquiry into the character and cost of public education in the State of New York.* New York: McGraw-Hill, 1938.

Srinivasan, J.T. Annual terminal examinations in the Jesuit high schools of Madras, India. Unpublished Ph.D. thesis. Boston College, 1971.

Tyler, R.W. The impact of external testing programs. In Findley, W.G. (Ed.), *The impact and improvement of school testing programs.* Chicago: National Society for the Study of Education, 1963, 193-210.

Chapter Nine

Competency Testing: Potential for Discrimination*

Merle Steven McClung

Introduction

In Palm Beach County, Florida, a group of parents organized an out-of-school tutoring program to help some eleventh grade students prepare for the Adult Performance Level (APL) Test to be given by the Palm Beach County Public Schools. The stakes were high. Students who passed the test by the time they graduated would be awarded the traditional high school diploma. Those who did not would have to settle for a "Certificate of Attendance," and this fact would be recorded on their high school transcript.[1]

The APL Test requires a fourth or fifth grade reading level and a seventh grade comprehension level, and requires the student "to apply accrued learning in 'real-life' situations."[2] The test may measure what the school never taught. One area superintendent stated that there had been "curriculum upheaval" during the last ten years, and basic skills were not stressed during that period.[3]

*From *Clearinghouse Review,* 1977, 439-448. Reprinted with permission of the author and publisher. Copyright © 1977 Legal Services Corp.

Furthermore, the school indicated that it would not guarantee that all of the objectives of the APL Test would be taught in 12 years of schooling.[4] No Spanish translation of the test had been planned up to this time.[5]

A shorter version of the test was given on a trial basis in 1976. Based on the 70 percent pass-fail cut-off score recommended by the Superintendent of Schools, 72 percent of the county's black students would have failed the test, but only 8.3 percent of the white students would have failed.[6] When the test was given with a 60 percent cut-off score,[7] nearly one out of every five juniors failed. The *Palm Beach Post-Times* reported: "A massive disparity between the performance of whites and nonwhites reflected in a trial run of the test last year was repeated with 42 percent or 576 minority children failing as opposed to eight percent or 252 white children."[8]

Palm Beach County is one of the many school systems that are in the forefront of the so-called "competency"[9] testing movement which is sweeping public education. The approach adopted by Palm Beach County was developed in response to a state-wide concern reflected in various educational accountability acts passed by the Florida Legislature since 1971.[10] The latest of these, The Educational Accountability Act of 1976,[11] required each school district by 1978-79 to establish standards for high school graduation that must include: (1) mastery of basic skills and satisfactory performance in functional literacy as designated by the state; and (2) completion of the minimum number of credits required by the district board of education. Each district is to provide for the awarding of differentiated diplomas to correspond with the varying achievement levels and competencies of graduates. The Act also required programs of pupil progression to be based upon performance by July 1, 1977—a provision designed to eliminate social promotions (the policy of promoting by age rather than achievement). Furthermore, a state-wide testing program is authorized to test students' basic skills in grades 3, 5, 8, and 11; the results are to be used to identify needs and to assess how well districts and schools are equipping students with the minimum skills necessary to function and survive in today's society.

State-wide assessment programs were first designed simply to measure performance in certain basic skills, with a purpose of identifying the school districts or individual schools in need of help. Extensive state-wide programs of this kind were adopted in Colorado,[12] Michigan,[13] New Jersey,[14] and other states, as well as Florida. The modest state-wide testing program authorized in Connecticut did not even permit identification by school district; it was designed instead to assess performance only by type of schools (for example, urban, suburban, and rural).[15] The trend of more recent legislation, however, has been to shift the burden of poor schooling onto the student by testing each student as an individual, with the demonstration of minimal competency in basic skills being a prerequisite to a high school diploma and/or grade-to-grade promotion. Oregon has led the way with the most extensive program of this kind currently being implemented.[16]

The Education Commission of the States reports[17] that during 1975-76, eight states[18] enacted competency testing legislation, and state boards of education in ten other states[19] issued rulings on the subject. Fifteen states[20] had legislation pending during 1977. In addition, many individual school districts, like Palm Beach County, have adopted their own minimal competency testing programs.[21] There is even a proposed bill before the U.S. Congress which would amend the Elementary and Secondary Education Act of 1965 to require all state agencies to establish a program of basic educational proficiency standards before they can receive funds under the Act.[22]

This emphasis on competency testing is, of course, a response to the widespread public dissatisfaction with the measurable outcome of public schooling. A number of studies indicates that, whatever definition of literacy is used, substantial numbers of Americans are not literate. One of the most recent of these studies, published by HEW, concluded that an estimated one million American youths 12 to 17 years old probably could not read as well as the average fourth grader, and thus could be called illiterate.[23] The study showed that disproportionate numbers of black youths were illiterate (3.2 percent).[24] Not surprisingly, the study also found the rate of illiteracy correlated with family income, declining from

14 percent in the lowest income group (less than $3,000) to 0.3 percent in the highest ($15,000).[25]

Some studies exaggerate the extent of illiteracy and incompetency among minority groups. An example is the widely publicized Adult Performance Level study[26] conducted by the University of Texas at Austin—the prototype for the Palm Beach APL Test.[27] The Texas study found that on overall competency performance in five knowledge and four skill areas, 19.7 percent of the population could be classified as "functionally incompetent" or "adults who function with difficulty," 33.9 percent could be classified as "functional adults," and 46.3 percent could be classified as "proficient adults."[28] The functional incompetency rate was 21.7 percent in reading, 16.4 percent in writing, and 32.9 percent in computation.[29] The study concluded: "Overall, approximately one-fifth of U.S. adults are functioning with difficulty."[30]

The Texas study also noted great differences between whites and minority groups. "While 16 percent of the whites are estimated to be functionally incompetent, about 44 percent of the black and 56 percent of the Spanish-surname groups are estimated to be so. Here, as with other variables that have been discussed, the differences are probably due to the relatively lower levels of income, education, job status, and job opportunity found among minority groups in this country."[31] This was only a partial explanation, however. The rate of minority incompetence was exaggerated by test norms which reflected middle-class standards of competence and ignored what might be called "ghetto survival skills." Cultural bias in the APL tests is discussed in more detail below in the section on racial discrimination.

These and other studies nevertheless identify serious shortcomings of many public schools in teaching basic skills. Although there may be no consensus about whether competency testing is the best means of remedying those shortcomings, few would disagree that care must be taken to assure that programs are designed and implemented in a fair and non-discriminatory manner.

The minimal competency requirement as a prerequisite to a high school diploma is a new phenomenon in most states;[32] it is, therefore, difficult to identify the strongest legal arguments for or against it and even more difficult to predict the judicial response. This chapter will identify a number of areas where competency testing programs may discriminate against students and will formulate some possible legal challenges against such discrimination.

The first inquiry about a competency test should be whether the test measures what was taught in school (that is, whether the test has "curriculum" and "instructional" validity, as defined below). If the test measures knowledge and/or skills which were never taught in school, then the test may violate substantive due process, because the school—rather than the students—are at fault and the students are being punished without being personally guilty. A strong Title VI claim is raised where disproportionate numbers of blacks or other minorities are adversely affected. If the test is also culturally or linguistically biased (that is, it is based upon and assumes a white middle-class background), the Title VI claim is greatly enhanced.

The argument is much more difficult, however, if the test does, in fact, measure what was taught in school because then the school board can argue that: (1) the test accurately reflects the student's achievement in mastering the curriculum; and (2) the board has a right as a matter of policy to establish a curriculum which reflects the dominant culture. The curriculum should, however, reflect all aspects of a pluralistic society (or at least the extent of diversity reflected by the student population). A curriculum which is biased against blacks or other minorities should be subject to a Title VI challenge.

The question of whether the test measures what was taught is relevant to either of two general purposes of competency testing: (1) measuring students' mastery of the school's curriculum; or (2) predicting the minimal competency required in the adult world.[33] The terminology will vary from school to school; some schools will merge the two concepts by deciding that their curriculum should be based upon minimal adult competency. Where an adult competency purpose is involved, the next question in analyzing the test should be whether the test is sufficiently predictive of minimal adult competency (that is, whether the test has "predictive" validity, as defined below). Depending upon the exact nature of the competency test, other types of validity may also be relevant. A competency test lacking predictive or some other type of validity when the test is based on assumptions of such validity may be so arbitrary as to violate substantive due process.

A further question raising the issue of fairness for all students, regardless of race, is whether the competency testing program has an adequate phase-in period. Two or three years' notice seems inadequate for a test measuring 12 years of cumulative learning; such notice may constitute a due process violation. The legal argument is stronger where the competency test requirement carries forward the effects of past racial discrimination, as would probably be the case in most formerly segregated school districts.

These problems and legal theories will be discussed in more detail by focusing first on: (1) racial discrimination; (2) inadequate phase-in periods; (3) tests which are not reliable or have not been validated; (4) inadequate matching of the instructional program to the test; (5) inadequate remedial instruction which creates or reinforces tracking; and (6) unfair apportionment of responsibility between students and educators.

Racial Discrimination

Some black parents in desegregated communities see a racial motive behind competency testing. They say that competency testing was not a concern at either black or white schools until the schools in their district were desegregated, at which time competency testing was introduced "to protect standards." The effect can be resegregation within the school according to test results (or other forms of tracking), since unequal educational opportunities may cause black children to score lower than their white counterparts.

Whether or not a racial motive is involved, such practices are arguably unconstitutional in formerly segregated districts, such as Palm Beach County. In comparable situations, the federal courts have held that practices which carry forward the effects of prior racial discrimination are prohibited. For example, the U.S.

Supreme Court in *Gaston County, N.C.* vs. *United States*,[34] an action brought under the Voting Rights Act of 1965, held that it was appropriate for a court to consider whether a literacy or educational requirement had the effect of denying the right to vote on account of race or color because the State had maintained separate and inferior schools for its black residents who are now of voting age. "[W]e cannot escape the sad truth that throughout the years Gaston County systematically deprived its black citizens of the educational opportunities it granted to its white citizens. 'Impartial' administration of the literacy test today would serve only to perpetuate these inequities in a different manner."[35]

Similarly, the Fifth Circuit Court of Appeals developed the standard that the testing necessary for ability grouping could not be applied to black students for the first time in years immediately following desegregation.[36] This "prior effects" principle arguably applies in other cases of serious injury, such as denial of grade promotion or a high school diploma.

The legal standard to be applied to other school districts (those not recently desegregated or found to be subject to prior discrimination) is less clear. As a constitutional matter, the Supreme Court held in *Washington* vs. *Davis*[37] that the disproportionate racial impact of a test (in this case, a police department's personnel test) was not sufficient to establish an unconstitutional racial classification without proof that it reflects a racially discriminatory purpose. The Court, however, stated that such disproportionate racial impact can be *evidence* of discriminatory purpose.[38]

In a concurring opinion, Justice Stevens noted that "the line between discriminatory purpose and discriminatory impact is not nearly as bright, and perhaps not quite as critical,"[39] as the majority's opinion suggested. "Frequently the most probative evidence of intent will be objective evidence of what actually happened rather than evidence describing the subjective state of mind of the actor. For, normally, the actor is presumed to have intended the natural consequence of his deeds."[40] Given the studies cited above, the natural consequence of most competency testing programs would be racial differentiation. In Palm Beach

County, the trial test offered additional evidence of the probable effect of the later test.

In *Washington* vs. *Davis,* the Supreme Court also distinguished between the constitutional standard and Title VII standard on testing, noting that the latter was more stringent since it incorporated an effect rather than a purpose standard.[41] Thus, when a test or practice disqualified substantially disproportionate numbers of blacks in hiring and promotion decisions, the burden under Title VII shifts to the employer to validate the test or practice in terms of job performance and to show that the test or practice is sufficiently job related.

The HEW regulations implementing Title VI of the Civil Rights Act of 1964 incorporate a similar effect (rather than purpose) standard, prohibiting practices which have the effect of discriminating against individuals on the ground of race, color, or national origin.[42] This Title VI effect standard has been cited with approval and applied by the U.S. Supreme Court in *Lau* vs. *Nichols.*[43] The Title VI regulations also incorporate the *Gaston County* principle[44] against carrying forward the effects of past discrimination, and add to it an affirmative obligation to take steps to remedy those effects.[45]

Application of these Title VI standards to public school testing programs is indicated by an HEW memorandum requiring schools to take steps "to adopt and implement procedures to insure that test materials and other assessment devices used to identify, classify, and place exceptional children are *selected and administered* in a manner which is *non-discriminatory in its impact* on children of any race, color, national origin, or sex . . ."[46] (italics added). Since virtually all public schools are subject to Title VI regulations, competency testing programs like that in Palm Beach County which have a disproportionate effect on blacks or other protected minorities should be examined in light of Title VI standards, especially where there is evidence of racial bias in the test itself or in the administration of the test.

Where competency testing programs have a disproportionate effect on Hispanic children, attorneys should also examine *Lau* vs. *Nichols*[47] and related HEW memoranda[48] requiring public schools to take affirmative steps to remedy the linguistic exclusion of non-English speaking children. The Palm Beach County school system has indicated that no Spanish translation of their competency test is planned at this time. Even a Spanish translation, however, without corresponding curricular and instructional modification, may not satisfy the HEW standards.[49]

The racial effect of the competency test comes about, in part, from cultural bias in the test. The different versions of APL tests and studies seek to measure an individual's ability to apply basic skills including literacy to adult life-role activities, such as consumer, producer, and citizen.[50] This measurement is used to determine "functional competency"; that is, an individual's ability to succeed in society. The higher rate of incompetency usually indicated for minorities by APL test scores is not surprising, since life-role knowledge as well as basic skills are being tested, and both aspects of the exam may be culturally biased.

The Texas APL Test, the prototype for the Palm Beach APL Test,[51] is culturally biased almost by definition, since the University of Texas researchers defined incompetent adults as those whose level of mastery of competency objectives is associated with "inadequate income of poverty level or less, inadequate education of eight years of school or fewer, and unemployment or low job status."[52] The researchers admit that functional competency is "a construct which is meaningful only in a specific societal context . . . . [it] is culture-bound."[53] The APL Test, thus, does not measure an individual's competence in functioning in that part of society in which he or she lives every day, but instead attempts to measure a person's competency by the test designer's conceptions of what is required for successful functioning in middle-class America. The ability to survive in a ghetto, for example, is not measured by the test, and therefore, the test results exaggerate the extent of functional incompetence among blacks and other minorities.

An APL Test guide[54] developed for the Palm Beach County Schools suggests that their APL Test is also culture-bound. The test guide includes many tasks which indicate a potential for discrimination in the test. For example, the "Consumer Economics" part of the test guide includes the following "comprehension" task: "To discuss the idea that just because a rich family can afford to feed, clothe, and educate a large number of children, this does not mean that the world will be able to support their children and grandchildren." One task in the "Occupational Knowledge" part asks students "to discuss proper behavior and attitudes for keeping a job." The "Health" part includes the following task: "To discuss the physical and psychological benefits gained when food is served attractively in a pleasant atmosphere." And one task in the "Government and Law" part asks students "to discuss the concept of party politics including why the two-party system has been successful."

Any functional competency test, and the curriculum on which the test is based, should reflect all aspects of a pluralistic society, or at least the extent of diversity reflected by the student population. A functional competency test given in the Miami or San Antonio public schools, for example, should include a number of Hispanic skill and content items, as some cross-cultural competence is arguably necessary for successful functioning as adults in those cities. In any case, a curriculum or competency test which is biased against blacks or Hispanics should be subject to a Title VI challenge.[55]

Inadequate Phase-In Periods

Many competency testing programs are being imposed upon students late in their secondary education with little prior notice. The Palm Beach juniors, for example, spent their first ten or eleven years in the school system without notice or knowledge that passing a competency test would be a condition to acquiring a diploma. The school system had, in fact, explicitly approved their progress by promoting them each year even though many of them did not have basic skill competencies. All prior classes of students had been graduated with diplomas without having to satisfy this additional requirement. It is likely that many, if not most, of these students failing the test would have studied (and teachers taught) differently in early years had they been given such notice. The competency test is designed to assure that minimal competency is acquired after 12 years of schooling, but Palm Beach juniors did not receive notice until their tenth year of schooling.

Traditional notions of due process should require adequate prior notice of any rule which could cause irreparable harm to a person's educational or occupational prospects.[56] *Mahavongsanan* vs. *Hall*[57] provides some support for the proposition that students must be provided with adequate notice of any significant change in graduation requirements, although the Fifth Circuit found that the plaintiff in that case had not been denied procedural or substantive due process because she received "timely notice" that passing a comprehensive examination would be a prerequisite to a master's degree in education.[58]

The legal argument for adequate notice of significant changes in graduation requirements is stronger in the context of elementary and secondary public schools than in postsecondary education because courts usually apply a stricter standard of review to practices at the elementary and secondary level where education is compulsory. Notice of a competency testing requirement for a high school diploma would have to be much earlier than in the *Mahavongsanan* case because twelve rather than just two or three years of education are being tested. The plaintiff in *Mahavongsanan* received notice of the new requirement relatively early in the program (only six months after starting the program), whereas Palm Beach juniors did not receive notice until their tenth year of schooling. Whatever notice is considered adequate in this situation (first grade? fourth grade?), notice after five-sixths of one's educational program is already completed seems clearly inadequate.

Reliability and Validity Problems

Even where students have been given adequate prior notice of the competency test requirement, the test itself may be discriminatory and illegal, if it does not meet certain standards. A basic understanding of psychological testing jargon is helpful in analyzing competency tests because courts have relied on this terminology in deciding other cases involving questions of fair testing.[59]

The courts have usually relied upon the *Standards for Educa-*

tional and Psychological Tests developed by the American Psychological Association (hereafter "APA Standards").[60] The APA Standards define the requirements for reliable and valid tests. Simply put, *reliability* refers to whether the instrument measures accurately what it measures (for example, the instrument should yield comparable results when used at different times).[61] *Validity* refers to whether the instrument measures what it purports to measure. There are many different kinds of test validity, as indicated below, and each should be considered in relation to the exact test in question. According to the APA Standards:

> Questions of validity are questions of what may properly be inferred from a test score . . . . [primarily] [w]hat can be inferred about what is being measured by the test [and] [w]hat can be inferred about other behavior? . . . . The kinds of validity depend upon the kinds of inferences one might wish to draw from test scores. Four interdependent kinds of inferential interpretation are traditionally described to summarize most test use: the *criterion-related* validities (*predictive* and *concurrent*); *content* validity and *construct* validity.[62]

Predictive validity is a measure of how well test items predict the future performance of test-takers. This type of assessment requires an analysis comparing the predictions about each test-taker based on the test results with the actual functioning of the test-taker at a later point in time. For example, if a high number of students which an APL test had predicted would be functionally incompetent in fact turned out to be such when studied years later, then the test could be said to have predictive validity.[63]

Concurrent validity is a measure of how well test results correlate with other criteria which might provide the same type of information about test-takers. This type of assessment provides a measure of a test's immediate predictive validity, or how well determinations based upon test results correlate with other currently available information about test-takers.[64]

Content validity is a measure of how well test items represent the knowledge that the test purports to measure. A test with a high degree of content validity is a test for which high test performance serves as an index of a high degree of skill or knowledge in the area which the test purports to measure.[65]

Construct validity is a measure of how well test items correlate to the theory or constructs behind the test. This assessment indicates the relationship between the theory behind the test and actual test performance. This assessment is probably the most difficult to conduct, since it may be difficult to identify the constructs upon which a test is built and because a statistical analysis of the interrelationship of test items may be required.[66]

The point here is not to attempt a technical evaluation of the APL Test itself, but rather to emphasize the need for such evaluation before this kind of test is used as a basis for promotion or graduation. In a carefully considered article on competency-based education, William Spady of the National Institute of Education draws attention to the technical obstacles to "reliable, valid, and timely measurement of applied role performance. The technology surrounding the assessment and measurement of success in life-role activities is only in its infancy, even though the rush toward adopting [competency-based] programs is upon us."[67] In addition to the concepts mentioned above, any technical evaluation of a competency test should also include an appraisal of its *curriculum* and *instructional* validity, as discussed in the next section.

Matching the Test with the Instruction

Most people would agree that fairness requires that a school's curriculum and instruction be matched in some way with whatever is later measured by the test. The test would be unfair if it measured what the school never taught. This concept is not included in the APA Standards,[68] but is of primary importance in considering the validity of any competency test.

Curriculum validity is a measure of how well test items represent the objectives of the curriculum to which the test-takers have been exposed.[69] An analysis of the curriculum validity of the Palm Beach APL Test would require a comparison of the APL objectives with the course objectives of the Palm Beach schools, as these objectives exist currently and existed during the years that this year's group of test-takers have been in school. If the curriculum is not and was not designed to teach functional competency, it is not appropriate to deny individual students their diploma because they did not learn to be functionally competent. In this situation, failure on the competency test should reflect on the schools, which are not offering an appropriate curriculum (assuming, of course, that the objectives, skills, and knowledge specified by the competency test are indeed appropriate curricular objectives for the particular school).

It would also seem appropriate to demand of any competency test another type of validity, which might be termed *instructional validity*.[70] Even if the curricular objectives for the school correspond with the competency test objectives, there must be some measure of whether or not the school district's stated objectives were translated into topics actually taught in the district's classrooms. Test items should measure topics taught. If test items do not reflect actual content of instruction, then the competency test should not be used as a high school graduation requirement for individual students, but rather as a general survey instrument to be employed in curriculum planning and development.[71] While a measure of curriculum validity is a measure of the theoretical validity of the competency test as an instrument to assess the success of students, instructional validity is an actual measure of whether the schools are providing students with instruction in knowledge and skills measured by the test. Thus, an analysis of the instructional validity of a competency test would require a comparison of the test items and objectives with actual course offerings in the school district.

A competency test measuring life skills and used as a basis for denying a diploma when such skills were never taught in the school is arguably so arbitrary as to violate due process of law.[72] A competency test lacking curriculum or instructional validity may also violate substantive due process because the *school* rather than the *student* can be faulted for poor performance on the test.

In an analogous case, the Fifth Circuit held that a school board regulation violated substantive due process because it allowed school children to be suspended for their parents' misconduct:

> [T]he children do not complain that they were denied the constitutional right to an education, but that they were punished without being personally guilty. Thus, a cardinal notion of liberty is involved and substantive due process is applicable.[73]

Since the practice established "a significant encroachment upon a basic element of due process," the Court required the school to meet "a substantial burden" to justify this encroachment, including proof that reasonable alternative means to achieve the stated objective were not available.[74]

There is evidence that the Palm Beach County APL Test lacks both curriculum and instructional validity. One area superintendent stated that basic skills were not stressed in the schools during ten years of curriculum upheaval. Perhaps many schools could show that their instructional programs have, in fact, been geared to the basic literacy skills measured by their versions of the competency test, but this may not be true of many "adult performance level" tests which measure content knowledge in addition to literacy. A somewhat different perspective on the same problem is provided by William Spady: "[T]he choice of goals may have a major impact on established instructional practices, particularly when life-role competencies imply exposure and activities that are either inadequately provided by or poorly simulated in classroom or formal school contexts and when teaching staff may lack the competence or versatility to facilitate certain goals."[75]

Inadequate Remedial Instruction

Some kind of remedial instruction should be provided as part of any competency testing program. Most competency testing programs, however, do not make adequate provision for any kind of instruction. "[I]n only eight states (California, Colorado, Georgia, Nebraska, New Jersey, Oregon, Pennsylvania, and Virginia) do either current or pending regulations seem to suggest that some kind of instructional experiences need to be provided students to facilitate their performance in desired outcome areas."[76] Florida should be added to this list because its statutes now provide:

> The first priority of the public schools of Florida shall be to assure that all Floridians, to the extent their individual physical, mental, and emotional capacities permit, shall achieve mastery of the basic skills.[77]

> Each district shall develop procedures for the remediation of [the deficiencies of] those students who are unable to meet such standards.[78]

The Florida legislature has also passed a bill providing limited funding for remedial programs,[79] but has not elaborated upon the kind of programs of instruction and remediation that are necessary. Important questions concerning the extent of local district commitment of time and resources are left unresolved. The Palm Beach program includes a summertime remedial component. This year's juniors will have three additional opportunities to pass the test. This would not appear, however, to provide either adequate remediation or adequate notice for a test of 12 years' cumulative learning.

A model program should provide for multiple evaluation, learning, and remedial opportunities.[80] It should create a continuing responsibility of the school and/or state to provide further remedial education and test opportunities at any point after leaving school for those former students who have sufficient motivation to try again to pass the test. A model program should also ensure that students who do not pass the test are not tracked in all courses just because some remedial instruction is necessary.[81] The legal limitations on tracking a disproportionate number of minority students have been summarized above.[82]

Apportionment of Responsibility

The shift in emphasis mentioned above from competency testing programs used to identify problem areas to competency testing which is a requirement for a high school diploma raises the question of whether the full burden of unsatisfactory performance should be placed on students. Learning is a two-way street with students and educators sharing joint responsibility.

Spady stresses "the central role of student performance data in the management and evaluation of all elements in the system" because "... students' performance in relation to outcome goals may be a reflection not only of their ability and endeavor but of the adequacy and appropriateness of the instruction provided, the evaluation tools used, or the goals themselves."[83] He also notes that "the delicate balance between student and system accountability" is usually overlooked by the states that are "jumping on a [competency-based] bandwagon under the assumption that toughening certification standards for students will satisfy the public's need for school system accountability."[84]

Similarly, it is interesting to note the apparent inconsistency of some teacher unions which argue that competency and other standardized testing should be used as one useful criterion (rather than the sole criterion) in assessing student performance, but should never be used even as one criterion in evaluating teacher performance (for example, tenure decisions).[85] This raises the question of what a model statute providing for joint responsibility would look like.

Broader Issues

The single-criterion assessment of students mentioned in the previous section raises broader questions. Single-criterion evaluation of students, teachers, and public education as a whole seems short-sighted. For one thing, the state of the art is not sufficiently developed to warrant such exclusive reliance on competency-based evaluations. Second, and more important, the primary goals of public education arguably are or should be broader than those reflected by minimal competencies, and students, teachers, and public education generally should not be evaluated exclusively by these narrow measures.

This issue is subject to considerable difference of opinion, as illustrated by California's early-exit program, which allows students to graduate from high school upon passing a minimal competency test.[86] It is also illustrated by the fully-based competency program projected by Spady.[87] Do such programs sell public education short? Even given a strong commitment to a broader view of public education, there is always the danger that the minimal standards will become maximums rather than minimums. As in other areas,[88] however, the need for establishing "minimum" standards has been demonstrated, and safeguards can be developed to assure that broader goals are not bypassed.

Competency-based education clearly raises many far-reaching issues. A comprehensive program would necessitate considerable restructuring of education, and would have important implications for grouping, student discipline, and other areas of public education which are too numerous and complex to be discussed in this chapter.[89] Any competency-based program also necessitates implicit or explicit decisions about performance objectives and educational goals. Given the crucial importance of these decisions, a model program should provide for representative community-based participation in the decision-making process.[90]

Conclusion

In discussing the potential for discrimination inherent in competency-based testing, this chapter has also suggested some provisions which might be included in any competency-based program designed to be administered fairly, with students and schools sharing responsibility for performance. At the very least, the basis for determining credit under an equitable competency program must, in Spady's words: "(1) be reflected in clear and specific criterion-referenced outcome statements that are (2) directly embodied in the instruction and evaluation of students and (3) known by them prior to their engagement in a given arena of work."[91]

As more and more states start to implement their versions of competency-based education, the potential unfairness of the programs, including but not limited to racial and socioeconomic discrimination, is becoming more apparent.

Notes

1. Questions and Answers Concerning the APL Test, at Answers 4-6, a five-page mimeographed statement prepared by the Palm Beach County Schools (January, 1977). [Hereinafter cited as Questions and Answers.]
2. *Ibid.*, at Answers 12, 13, and 16.
3. *Palm Beach Post-Times,* April 3, 1977.
4. Questions and Answers, *supra* note 1, at Answer 21.
5. *Ibid.*, at Answer 11.
6. *Supra* note 3.
7. Under Florida's Educational Accountability Act of 1976, Fla. School Laws (1976 ed.). Ch. 229.55 *et seq.,* local districts have discretion to determine the cut-off score. The Florida Department of Education is proposing different standards for each county based on a formula of expected

achievement of students in each county. The absence of a single state-wide standard has been criticized as a "loop-hole" in the law. See, e.g., Editor, *Educators Shouldn't Spoil Testing System,* Tallahassee Democrat, June 7, 1977.

8. *Palm Beach Post-Times,* May 10, 1977.

9. Since the legal analysis is essentially the same, this chapter uses the term "competency testing" in a general sense to mean tests purporting to measure basic skills and or life-role activities. More exact terminology is offered by William Spady, who defines "*competencies* as indicators of successful performance in life-role activities (be they producer, consumer, political citizen, driver, family member, intimate friend, recreational participant, or life-long learner) and distinguishes them from the discrete cognitive, manual, and social *capacities* (such as reading and computational skills, speaking ability, and motivation) that, when integrated and adopted to particular social contexts, serve as the *enablers* or *building blocks* on which competencies ultimately depend." W. Spady, *Competency-Based Education: A Bandwagon in Search of a Definition,* ED., RESEARCHER, at p. 10 (January, 1977). [Hereinafter cited as *Competency-Based Education.*] The terms "proficiency" and "basic skills" are often used in the same sense as "capacities."

10. For a discussion of the Educational Accountability Act of 1971, Title 15, Florida Statutes, S.229.57, and subsequent revisions, *see* the Cooperative Accountability Project's *Educational Accountability in Four States: Colorado, Connecticut, Florida, and Michigan,* at pp. 8-9 (December, 1975), available from the Education Commission of the States, Denver, Colo. [Hereinafter cited as *Educational Accountability.*]

11. *See* Florida School Laws (1976 ed.) Ch. 229.55 *et seq.,* especially Ch. 229.814, 230.2311, and 232.24.

12. Educational Accountability Act of 1971, Colorado Revised Statutes (1971), Title 22, Art. 7 at Sec. 123-41-1 *et seq.,* discussed and reprinted in *Educational Accountability, supra* note 10 at pp. 3-7, 96-104, and throughout the report.

13. Pub. Act No. 38 (1970), Vol. 18, Mich. C.L.A. Sec. 388. 1081-1086, is discussed and reprinted in *Educational Accountability, supra* note 10 at pp. 10-11, 108-109, and throughout the report.

14. Public School Education Act of 1975, New Jersey Statutes, Ch. 212, Laws of 1975, discussed and reprinted in Cooperative Accountability Project, *Legislation by the States: Accountability and Assessment in Education,* at pp. 7, 13-22 (December, 1975).

15. Pub. Act No. 665 (1971), Conn. Gen. Stat. Sec. 10-4, discussed and reprinted in *Educational Accountability, supra* note 10 at pp. 7-8, 105, and throughout the report.

16. *See* Oregon Administrative Rules: Minimum Standards (June, 1976), available from Oregon State Department of Education.

17. Education Commission of the States. Update V: Minimal Competency Testing (C. Pipho ed., April 20, 1977), 30 pp.

18. *Ibid.*, California, Colorado, Florida, Maryland, New Jersey, Virginia, Washington, and Louisiana.

19. *Ibid.*, Arizona, Georgia, Delaware, Michigan, Missouri, Nebraska, New York, Oregon, Vermont, and Idaho.

20. *Ibid.*, Alabama, Arizona, Arkansas, California, Florida, Illinois, Kansas, Maine, Massachusetts, Minnesota, Nevada, North Carolina, South Carolina, Iowa, and Maryland.

21. *Ibid.*

22. H. Rep. No. 6088, introduced by Representative Ronald M. Mott (D), would amend Title VII of the Elementary and Secondary Education Act to require states to establish a program of basic educational proficiency standards in reading, writing, and mathematics as a condition to receive federal assistance under the Act. A National Commission on Basic Education would be established to review state plans and set standards. The bill does not address the notice and discrimination problems which are the subject of this chapter.

23. PUB. HEALTH SERVICE, LITERACY AMONG YOUTHS 12-17 YEARS, at p. 3 (December, 1973), HEW Pub. No. (HRA) 74-1613.

24. *Ibid.*, at p. 4.

25. *Ibid.*, at p. 6.

26. The University of Texas at Austin, Adult Functional Competency: A Summary (March, 1975) (Dr. Norwell Northcutt, Project Director). [Hereinafter cited as Texas Study.]

27. The Texas research was turned over to the American College Testing Program (ACT) of Iowa City, Iowa, a test developer and publisher. ACT publishes an "Adult APL Survey" and a "Secondary School APL Survey." In the Fall of 1977, ACT began to market tests in each of the five content areas discussed below plus tests tailored to specifications provided by school districts. Palm Beach County Public Schools entered into a contract with ACT whereby an APL test was formulated for the school district.

28. Texas Study, *supra* note 26 at p. 6.

29. *Ibid.*

30. *Ibid.*

31. *Ibid.*, at p. 8.

32. Compare new competency testing legislation discussed in this chapter with Regents Examination in New York State (3a Sec. CIS. Education Law, Sec. 208 *et seq.*).

33. Compare these two purposes with Spady's distinction between *capacities* and *competencies* at *supra* note 9.

34. 89 S.Ct. 1720 (1969). *See also* Oregon vs. Mitchell, 91 S.Ct. 260 (1970); Kirksey vs. Board of Supervisors of Hinds County, Miss., No. 75-2212 (5th Cir. 1977), *reversing* 528 F.2d 536 (5th Cir. 1976).

35. 89 S.Ct. 1720, at 1726 (1969).
36. McNeal vs. Tate County School Dist., 508 F.2d 1017 (5th Cir. 1975); Moses vs. Washington Parish School Bd., 456 F.2d 1285 (5th Cir. 1972); Lemon vs. Bossier Parish School Bd., 444 F.2d 1400 (5th Cir. 1971); Singleton vs. Jackson Municipal School Dist., 419 F.2d 1211 (5th Cir. 1969).
37. 96 S.Ct. 2040 (1976).
38. *Ibid.*, at p. 2049.
39. *Ibid.*, at p. 2054.
40. *Ibid.*
41. *Ibid.*, at p. 2051.
42. Title VI, Sec. 601 of the Civil Rights Act of 1964 states that "No person in the United States shall, on the ground of race, color, or national origin, be excluded from participation in, be denied the benefits of, or be subjected to discrimination under any program or activity receiving Federal financial assistance." Regulations issued by the Department of HEW pursuant to this section states that a recipient of federal funds "may not . . . utilize criteria or methods of administration which have *the effect* of subjecting individuals to discrimination because of their race, color, or national origin, or have the effect of defeating or substantially impairing accomplishment of the objectives of the program as respect individuals of a particular race, color, or national origin." (italics added) 45 C.F.R. Sec. 80.3(b) (2). Other parts of the regulations particularly relevant to competency testing programs include the following:

In federally-affected area assistance . . . for general support of the operation of elementary or secondary schools . . . discrimination by the recipient school district in any of its elementary or secondary schools in the . . . treatment of its students in any aspect of the educational process, is prohibited, 45 C.F.R. Sec. 80.5(b).

A recipient under any program to which this part applies may not, directly or through contractual or other arrangements, on the ground of race, color, or national origin . . . (iv) Restrict an individual in any way in the enjoyment of any advantage or privilege enjoyed by others receiving any service, financial aid, or other benefit under the program . . . (v) Treat an individual differently from others in determining whether he satisfies any admission, enrollment, quota, eligibility, membership, or other requirement or condition which individuals must meet in order to be provided any service, financial aid, or other benefit provided under the program . . . 45 C.F.R. Sec. 80.3(b).

43. 94 S.Ct. 786, 789 (1974).
44. *See* text relating to *supra* note 35.
45. 45 C.F.R. Part 80.3(b) (6) (i) provides:

In administering a program regarding which the recipient has previously discriminated against persons on the ground of race, color, or national origin, the recipient must take affirmative action to overcome the effects of prior discrimination. 45 C.F.R. Part 80.5 provides the following illustrations of prohibited discrimination:

(i) in some situations, even though the past discriminatory practices attributable to a recipient or applicant have been abandoned, the consequences of such practices continue to impede the full availability of a benefit. If the efforts required of the . . . recipient . . . have failed to overcome these consequences, it will become necessary . . . for such . . . recipient to take additional steps to make the benefits fully available to racial and nationality groups previously subjected to discrimination . . .

(j) even though an applicant or recipient has never used discriminatory policies, the services and benefits of the program or activity it administers may not, in fact, be equally available to some racial or nationality groups. In such circumstances, an applicant or recipient may properly give special consideration to race, color, or national origin to make the benefits of its program more widely available to such groups, not then being adequately served . . .

46. HEW Memorandum by OCR Director, M. Gerry, Identification of Discrimination in the Assignment of Children to Special Education (August, 1975).

47. 94 S.Ct. 786 (1974).

48. HEW Memorandum by OCR Director, J. Pottinger. Identification of Discrimination and Denial of Services on the Basis of National Origin (May 25, 1970). *See also* subsequent memoranda, Evaluation of Voluntary Compliance Plans . . . (Summer, 1975), and Application of Lau Remedies (April 8, 1976).

49. A claim of linguistic discrimination could also be based upon 20 U.S.C. Sec. 1703(f) which provides that "No state shall deny equal educational opportunity to an individual on account of his or her race, color, sex, or national origin, by . . . (f) the failure by an educational agency to take appropriate action to overcome language barriers that impede equal participation by its students in its instructional program"; and 20 U.S.C. Sec. 1706 which provides that "an individual denied an equal educational opportunity . . . may institute a civil action in an appropriate district court of the United States against such parties, and for such relief, as may be appropriate."

50. For the range of competency (*i.e.,* outcome) expectations reflected in various competency testing programs, *see* W. Spady and D. Mitchell, *Competency-Based Education: Organizational Issues and Implications,* ED., RESEARCHER (February, 1977). [Hereinafter cited as Spady and Mitchell.]

51. See *supra* note 27.

52. Texas Study, *supra* note 26 at p. 5.

53. *Ibid.,* at p. 2.

54. A Note Concerning APL Goals, Objectives, and Tasks (March, 1975), 37 pp.

55. Under Title VI, the curriculum as well as other parts of the school program should not be designed in such a way as to exclude minority children from the benefits of participating in federally funded educational programs. *See, e.g.,* United States vs. Texas, 330 F. Supp. 235, 249 (E.D. Tex. 1971); Morgan vs. Kerrigan, 401 F. Supp. 216, 234 (D. Mass., 1975) where courts ordered non-discriminatory curricula as part of school desegregation plans.

56. The legal standard applied in modern substantive due process cases (under the Fourteenth Amendment of the U.S. Constitution or comparable state due process provisions) is usually not spelled out very carefully, but these cases usually invalidate state action which (1) is arbitrary or capricious, (2) does not achieve any legitimate state interests, (3) frustrates any legitimate interest the state might have, or (4) is fundamentally unfair. *See, e.g.,* discussion and cases cited in McClung, *The Problem of the Due Process Exclusion,* 3 J. OF LAW & ED., 491, 495-501 (October, 1974), and subsequent cases cited in the EDUCATION LAW BULLETIN published by the Center for Law and Education, Sec. 185. Whatever the exact wording of the test under substantive due process, the general standard is that state action cannot be unreasonable, with unreasonableness being construed narrowly (*e.g.,* rational persons would not disagree).

57. 529 F.2d 448 (5th Cir. 1976).

58. Further research in education and analogous areas (welfare, social security, etc.) may turn up cases with more careful discussion of notice requirements in non-criminal public programs.

59. Court involvement in determinations of test validity has focused primarily on situations involving employee selection procedures and on questions of predictive validity or adequate alternatives thereto. *See, e.g.,* Washington vs. Davis, 96 S.Ct. 2040 (1976), a case involving a challenge to testing practices followed by the Washington, D.C. police department in selecting individuals for its training academy. The majority opinion at footnote 13 notes the following cases involving the validation of employment tests: Albemarle Paper Co. vs. Moody, 422 U.S. 405, 431 (1975); Douglas vs. Hampton, 512 F.2d 976, 984 (D.C. Cir. 1975); Vulcan Society vs. Civil Service Comm'n, 490 F.2d 387, 394 (2nd Cir. 1973).

Also, the same footnote indicates that the standard followed in those cases, as well as that relied upon by the Equal Employment Opportunity Commission in fashioning its Guidelines on Employment Selection Procedures, 29 C.F.R. Sec. 1607, is the standard set forth in AMERICAN PSYCHO-LOGICAL ASSOC., STANDARDS FOR EDUCATIONAL AND PSYCHO-LOGICAL TESTS AND MANUAL (1966) (revised and renamed in 1971).

60. *Ibid.*

61. *See* AMERICAN PSYCHOLOGICAL ASSOC., STANDARDS FOR EDUCATIONAL AND PSYCHOLOGICAL TESTS, at 49 *et seq.* (1971).

[Hereinafter **APA STANDARDS.**] In other words, the *reliability* of a test is its trustworthiness, the stability and consistency of test results over time, and the accuracy of the test score in relation to a test-taker's "true score" if the test were a perfect indicator. This assessment is conducted by administering the same test more than once to the same group of test-takers, by administering alternate forms of the same test to the same group of test-takers at two separate times, or by administering in immediate succession two different forms of the test to the test-takers. In each case, statistical comparisons of results on each administration of the test are made.

62. APA STANDARDS, *supra* note 61 at pp. 25-26.

63. *For example,* an analysis of the predictive validity of the Palm Beach APL would require administration of the test to a group of high school-aged students with each student being given a score which could be interpreted as a prediction of the student's future "functional competency" as an adult. Then, the same group of students would be looked at several years later to determine, on the basis of each student's attained economic and educational status, whether the prediction was correct. *See* APA STANDARDS, *supra* note 61 at pp. 26-28.

64. *For example,* an analysis of the concurrent validity of the Palm Beach APL would require that test results on this year's administration of the test be compared with other current information available about the test-takers which is similar. This comparison might be made by determining the degree of correlation between the test scores and students' grades. However, this comparison would only be meaningful if student grades were a measure of academic achievement only (and did not include, for example, some weighting of "good conduct," "effort," etc.). Also, the comparison would be meaningful only if the curriculum actually provided instruction on the topics covered by the APL test (*see* the discussion of curriculum and instructional validity *infra*.).

65. *For example,* an analysis of the content validity of the Palm Beach APL would require a comparison of the test items with the skills and knowledge defined as necessary for "functional competency" to assess whether or not the test items can logically be said to be measures of that skill and knowledge. *See* APA STANDARDS, *supra* note 61 at p. 28.

66. *For example,* an analysis of the construct validity of the Palm Beach APL would require "the formulation of hypotheses about the characteristics of those who have high scores on the test in contrast to those who have low scores. Taken together, such hypotheses form at least a tentative theory about the nature of the construct the test is believed to be measuring. . . Such hypotheses of theoretical formulations lead to certain predictions about how people at different score levels on the test will behave on certain other tests or in certain defined situations. If the investigator's theory about what the test measured is essentially correct, most of his or her predictions should be confirmed." *Ibid.,* at p. 30. It would appear that the constructs behind the

original APL test were that there are certain skills and knowledge essential for success as a competent adult and that these can be measured on a two-dimensional model which simultaneously assesses skills and content knowledge. *Id.*

67. *Competency-Based Education, supra* note 9 at p. 11: *see also* George Madaus and Peter Airasian, *Issues in Evaluating Student Outcomes in Competency-Based Graduation Programs.* J. OF RES. & DEV. IN ED., 79-91 (Spring, 1977).

68. The APA limits its discussion of validity standards to consideration of the concepts of criterion-related validity, content validity, and construct validity. Most probably, this limitation occurs because the standards are promulgated primarily to regulate the conduct of organizations which develop and market tests and organizations which purchase those tests. Also, the standards are written by test designers and institutional users. These two factors may explain why the APA Standards do not include some considerations which are important to test-takers.

69. W. Dick & N. Hagerty, TOPICS IN MEASUREMENT: RELIABILITY AND VALIDITY, at p. 96 (1971); and L. Cronbach, ESSENTIALS OF PSYCHOLOGICAL TESTING, at p. 397 (1960).

70. The discussion in this chapter of the various types of test validity was developed with the assistance of Diana Pullin, Center for Law and Education. Since neither the APA Standards nor the educational literature generally seem to address the issue of matching the test with actual instruction (especially important in the fair administration and assessment of any minimal competency program), the concept of "instructional validity" was developed for this purpose by the author. Instructional validity obviously does not require prior exposure of the student to the exact questions asked on the test, but it does require actual exposure of students to the kind of knowledge and skills which would enable a student to answer the test questions. This will present difficult proof problems in some cases; in others, it will be easy to show that the test is measuring what the school never taught.

71. ACT, *supra* note 27, states that their "Adult APL Survey" and "Secondary School APL Survey" were designed "to be used primarily as aids in curriculum planning and development or in the determination of the need for additional instruction." AMERICAN COLLEGE TESTING PROG., USER'S GUIDE: ADULT APL SURVEY, at p. 2 (1976).

72. *See supra* note 56.

73. St. Ann vs. Palisi, 495 F.2d 423, 426 (5th Cir. 1974).

74. *Ibid.*, at pp. 426-27.

75. *Competency-Based Education, supra* note 9 at p. 11. For a complete description of the ways in which conventional curriculum and instruction are not well matched with competency-based tests, *see*, Spady and Mitchell, *supra* note 50 at pp. 9-10, 13.

76. Spady and Mitchell, *supra* note 50 at p. 13.

77. Fla. School Laws, Ch. 230.2311(1) (1976 ed.).
78. Fla. School Laws, Ch. 232.245(3) (1976 ed.).
79. The Florida Compensatory Education Act of 1977, S.B. No. 30-A (1977), signed by the Governor on June 23, 1977, provides ten million dollars for this purpose. The amount is inadequate in view of the numbers of students needing compensatory programs.
80. *See Competency-Based Education, supra* note 9 at p. 10.
81. Compensatory programs can be integrated or coordinated with regular programs so that students needing such help are not separated and stigmatized by a separate track.
82. *See* text relating to *supra* note 36.
83. *Competency-Based Education, supra* note 9 at p. 12.
84. *Ibid.*, at p. 12 and p. 13.
85. *See, e.g.,* the results of a survey of the American Federation of Teachers (AFT) Task Force on Educational Issues reported in Bhaerman, *What Do Teachers Think About Tests and Testing?,* AMERICAN EDUCA-TOR, at p. 14 (Winter, 1977).
86. S.B. No. 1112 (1972) and S.B. No. 1243 (1975) provide for the California High School Proficiency Test. Upon successful completion of the test, 16- and 17-year-old students may be awarded a proficiency certificate legally equivalent to a high school diploma. They may leave high school if they pass the test and receive parental permission. S.B. No. 1502, Ch. 315 (1976) changes the "early out" minimal competency test program by making it available to citizens over the age of 18. Another act, A.B. No. 3408, Ch. 856 (1976) requires districts to establish proficiency standards, and provides that no student can receive a high school diploma after June, 1980, unless the student passes a proficiency test.
87. A fully-based competency program would eliminate attendance and other criteria for grading and rely exclusively on demonstration of competency. *See Competency-Based Education, supra* note 9 at p. 12. Such a program, however, does not necessarily imply narrow goals and performance objectives subject to the limitations of quantifiable measurement. *Ibid.*, at p. 14, n.6.
88. *For example,* compare bar and medical examinations or examinations for driver's licenses.
89. *For example,* Spady notes that competency-based education can "fundamentally undermine the potential use of evaluation (testing and grades) as a mechanism for the control of student behavior. . . The use of assignments or tests as surprises or threats is dramatically reduced when . . . the expectations for performance are clear and known by students in advance." *Competency-Based Education, supra* note 9 at p. 12. For more detailed discussion, see Spady and Mitchell, *supra* note 50 at pp. 11-14.
90. Community representation is required under many state accountability statutes, but the nature and extent of representation is not often specified. *See, e.g.,* New Jersey's statute, *supra* note 14.
91. *Competency-Based Education, supra* note 9 at p. 10.

Chapter Ten

Costs in Minimal
Competency Testing Programs

Peter W. Airasian
George F. Madaus
Joseph J. Pedulla
Kenneth B. Newton

With expenditures for education already amounting to approximately eight percent of the nation's gross national product, and per pupil expenditures increasing by roughly 50 percent (adjusted for inflation) over a ten-year period, costs become a determining factor in both the acceptance and design of new programs. Interestingly, in spite of large cost increases for education in the past decade, one 1976 poll indicated that 52 percent of the American public thinks too *little* money is being spent on education. Only ten percent responded "too much," and the remaining 38 percent indicated the amount being spent was "about right." It does not follow, however, that the American public is willing to translate these opinions into action. Consider that in the decade 1965-1975, both the absolute number and the percentage of school bond referendums approved by the public dropped noticeably. About 75 percent of such bond proposals won approval in 1964-65, compared to fewer than half in

1974-75. Monies approved dropped from $2.5 billion to $1.2 billion in the same period, despite inflation of the dollar. This trend may imply that the public is not willing to contribute to increased local expenditures for schools but prefers that the increases come from the state and federal level. Indeed, an informal poll of teachers, administrators, parents, and students taken in conjunction with public meetings on Minimal Competency Testing conducted by the Bureau of Research and Assessment in the Commonwealth of Massachusetts indicated that about 80 percent of the 464 respondents felt that local school districts should pay none or only some of the costs of a minimal competency program. Thus, the policy-maker must consider not only the absolute costs of a minimal competency program but the source of funding as well.

It seems fortunate that the perceived desire for state-funded programs would also result in some cost reductions due to economies of scale. However, the cost issue is unlikely to be resolved quite this easily, because there are undesirable and intangible costs associated with a centralized program which can reduce the grass-roots support for a state controlled minimal competency program. Such support is, of course, vital to the success of any such program.

There is a broad range of costs associated with minimal competency testing programs. Some costs are obvious, such as test development; others are less obvious, such as legal costs in defending against lawsuits. In addition to monetary costs, there are also intangible costs, such as teacher dissatisfaction or local antagonism toward state mandated programs. The remainder of this chapter is divided into three sections. First, a brief explication of possible costs is presented. For the purposes of this discussion, costs are classified into four general categories: (1) program development costs; (2) administration and implementation costs; (3) costs associated with the consequences and results of testing; and (4) intangible costs. Most of the costs identified below will have to be met regardless of the eventual format of the minimal competency program. In the second section, some of the factors which influence the magnitude of the costs are discussed. It is important to note that many of these factors have different effects on cost categories. An attempt to reduce one type of cost by manipulation of a particular factor may well tend to cause an increase in another cost category. For example, attempts to reduce administration and implementation costs may result in an increase in the costs associated with the consequences and results of testing. In the final section, an effort is made to quantify some of the costs associated with a minimal competency testing program. Where possible, dollar estimates of specific costs are provided.

Possible Costs

Program development. The word "development" suggests the process of test development, but this is only the most obvious of a set of developmental costs related to minimal competency testing programs. For many people, tests are the focus of such programs, but in a very real sense, tests are only tools to facilitate decision-making. Within school systems, program development involves the preparation of both students and staff for the implementation of the program. Moreover, use of the word "development" tends to be linked to the idea of one-time costs; however, many developmental costs will be ongoing, albeit at a reduced level, if the program is to be maintained and updated.

At least six specific costs fall under the rubric of program development:

1. *Competency identification and codification.* This process can be long and complex, involving widespread information gathering at the outset, and concerted efforts by teams of "experts" at refining the statement of competencies to be included in the program. Regardless of the route taken, competencies must be identified, operationalized, and disseminated, hopefully with a spirit of consensus. All of this costs time and money.

2. *Curriculum development/modification.*
   a. From the identified competencies to be tested, behavioral objectives need to be developed both as a basis for instruction and as a basis for testing.
   b. Curriculum in the form of guides, lesson plans, course outlines, or "planned course statements" similar to those developed for Oregon's competency program, may have to be produced.

3. *Public relations.* At the very least, the public must be informed of the nature and purposes of the program. The Oregon example illustrates that this may be accomplished along with curriculum development. Not only do the Oregon "planned course statements" serve as curriculum guides but as information for the public as well.

4. *Inservice training.* There may be a need to train staff in the administration and/or interpretation of the test results. In any event, staff time will be required for instruction and providing information regarding the implementation of the program. Inservice training can become especially important and expensive in those cases where the minimal competencies include areas or skills not currently emphasized in most school curricula, for example, certain oral or aural skills.

5. *Test development.* Regardless of the manner of test development, local, state, or commercial, there are costs associated with it. If an already available test were to be used, these costs might be labeled procurement costs and would be very much an ongoing concern. Subsumed in test development costs are the costs of pilot-testing which would be required regardless of the test to be used. If a new test must be developed each year, there will be yearly test development costs.

6. *Test validation.* As an adjunct to development costs, there may be substantial costs associated with test validation, especially in the case of indirect, paper-and-pencil measures. Even if development costs are circumvented by using already available standardized tests, one could still incur costs in validating the test for a particular use and situation.

Administration and implementation. As with costs in the development stage, there are additional costs associated with the administration and implementation of a program other than those associated with the mere administration of tests. Clearly, most of the costs involved at this stage are of an ongoing nature and hold relatively constant year after year. Six examples of such costs follow:

1. *Test administration including scoring.* The costs obviously vary widely depending on many factors: type of test, frequency of administration, number of grade levels involved, machine- or

hand-scoring, etc. Anderson (1977) has noted that there is a possibility for cost benefits here. For example, if tests could be administered to large groups of students by clerical personnel, the teaching staff may be free for other tasks during testing periods.

2. *Record keeping.* Virtually all the local districts and states which have experiences with competency testing programs report record keeping as a major problem and concern. It is conceivable that new staff may be required here depending on the complexity of records desired. Demonstrating instructional validity may require quite extensive long-term record keeping.

3. *Enforcement.* A strong word, perhaps, but compliance with a testing program is by no means automatic. There is a legal concern here; the more important the decisions to be made on the basis of competency tests, the more important compliance becomes. There may have to be a vehicle developed for enforcing compliance.

4. *Monitoring.* Apart from enforcement concerns, the regulating agency, state or local, has an obvious need to monitor the operation of a testing program and insure its responsiveness to changing concerns.

5. *Provisions for special needs and bilingual students.* If the decision is made, as seems likely, that special tests are needed for some students in these categories, then alternative methods of assessing their competencies will have to be employed. Almost certainly, these methods will be more expensive on a per pupil basis than the regular tests, especially if the regular minimal competency test is the paper-and-pencil variety.

6. *Additional staff.* Depending on the nature of the program, there may be a need for new staff for test development, interpretation, and inservice needs.

Consequences and results. The costs of a minimal competency program do not stop once the test scores are in. In fact, one of the major cost concerns expressed by those working with such programs is the cost of compensatory/remedial programs for those pupils who fail the test. Several of the costs associated with the period after testing are briefly discussed below.

1. *Remediation/compensatory programs.* Here again, there is an underlying legal concern. To the extent that important educational

decisions will be made on the basis of minimal competency tests, there is a legal responsibility to provide not only the instruction in the first instance, but also remediation for those pupils who fail. Legal issues aside, presumably the goal of minimal competency programs is not to weed children out and save the fittest, but rather to insure that as many children as possible attain the competencies. This goal will almost certainly require remedial programs. It is entirely possible that additional staff may be required to provide remedial instruction, particularly at the secondary level.

2. *Legal.* Perhaps, unfortunately, it is likely that lawsuits will grow out of minimal competency programs, possibly in the form of so-called educational malpractice suits. Such suits involve direct defense costs as well as indirect costs. In the latter category, for example, are record keeping costs referred to above. Accurate individual records of when specific competencies were taught may be legal money in the bank.

3. *Reallocation of resources.*
   a. From the gifted and average student to the low achiever. More resources may have to be devoted to low achievers than is already the case in many districts.
   b. From enrichment courses to core or basic courses. It seems almost unavoidable that if basics (as defined by the accepted competencies) are to be the focus of new programs, other courses, e.g., art, music, foreign languages, social studies, science, may experience a decrease in financial support.

4. *Dissemination of information.* The public will want to know the results of minimal competency testing. Information will have to go out on two levels: to the public at large about the overall performance and to individual parents about their children's performance. The information required will likely require more than merely reporting scores and will involve some guidance on how the results are to be construed and interpreted.

Intangibles. Costs in this category are by their very nature difficult to identify, to anticipate, to describe, and to quantify. Yet, they are real and can scuttle a program more easily than monetary costs. Most of these costs are related to attitudes and practices of the staff and clientele of the school system. A minimal competency program is doomed to failure without the support of these people. Fortunately, several of the costs identified below might be better characterized as risks. To the extent that these risks are identified, anticipated, and planned for, their costs can be held to a minimum. Nine examples of intangible costs are:

1. *State-local district polarization.* As noted above, economies of scale may indicate a centralized testing program as the economical way to go. Furthermore, the general public probably favors funding flowing from somewhere other than the local level. However, if a minimal competency program is conceived, developed, and implemented from the state level, there may be a real risk of lack of local support for the program. Organizational theory posits that change is most likely to succeed when those individuals who are most affected by the change participate in defining the problem, setting the goals and standards, and developing alternative strategies for implementation.

2. *Local administration-teaching staff polarization.* The same concern discussed in (1) above may be a problem at the local level as well, depending on whether the teaching staff sense "ownership" of the program or whether they sense it as forced upon them from school administration. The risks here are of teacher dissatisfaction, antipathy, and complaints of being overburdened. Unless teachers fully support the program, it might well become a collective bargaining issue as well.

3. *Public dissatisfaction with school results.* Although there is apparently a public call for competency testing, such a program will not be a panacea for whatever ills have generated the call. Public expectations, however, might be very high, and if the results do not live up to expectations immediately, the public will likely be unhappy.

4. *Antagonism from parents whose children fail.* There is a very real philosophical and legal question over who should be held accountable for the attainment of competencies; the child, the teacher, the school, the school system, etc. One thing is certain: most parents will hold someone other than their children accountable. Therefore, parents of children who fail competency tests form a public with a real potential for antagonism toward the schools.

5. *Self-concept of pupils who fail.* The whole notion of social promotion now called into question by some competency testing proponents is predicated on avoiding stigmatizing children. A minimal competency test with a clearly defined cut-off point holds

the possibility of labeling children to their detriment. As with certain other costs, the more important the educational decisions to be made based on a competency test, the greater the risk involved in damaging a child's self-concept.

6. *Lowering standards to the minimal competencies.* Many existing programs tied to graduation require performance at an eighth grade level in order to pass. There is a danger that the level of competency required by the test becomes maximal, rather than minimal; the ceiling rather than the floor for educators and pupils.

7. *Less effort put into non-core subjects.* In addition to the monetary reallocations noted above, non-core courses may also suffer from intangible losses in pupil, staff, and public attention and support.

8. *How will private/parochial school pupils be handled?* Will their pupils be required to pass tests in order to receive a high school diploma? If the answer is no, there may be repercussions from parents in both the public and private sectors.

9. *Effects on existing programs.* If remediation is a mandated activity, will existing Title I funds be curtailed on the basis of the argument that Title I funds are not intended to be used for mandated programs within districts? If various categories of "special need" pupils are excluded from a minimal competency program, will this exemption become an escape clause for many and increase diagnostic and remedial costs?

Factors Influencing the Magnitude of Costs

It should be obvious that the costs of a minimal competency testing program vary in their impact. Many of the costs identified above may be either negligible or prohibitively expensive. For example, the cost of administering a test has a recognized range of from 15 cents per pupil to $13 per pupil (Anderson, 1977); the former being a figure cited by Denver authorities as the cost of administering their competency tests, the latter a figure associated with a secure certification test administered by a private contractor. Policy-makers should be aware that the general magnitude of costs is largely determined by the *a priori* decisions they make about the purposes and design of their program. In this section, we shall briefly discuss some of the decisions which impact greatly on costs. The decisions concern the following factors:

(1) the model chosen;
(2) type of test;
(3) number of competencies to be tested;
(4) nature of the decisions to be made based on the testing program;
(5) the percent of pupils one is willing to fail;
(6) the percent of pupils who are expected to master the competencies;
(7) the difficulty of the competencies; and
(8) frequency of testing.

The minimal competency testing model one chooses to implement influences costs in several different ways. The main feature of the model which influences costs is the degree of state involvement. In general, it appears that some tangible costs decrease with state involvement due to economies of scale and centralization of tasks, while some intangible costs may rise due to weakened local support for a state-developed and administered program. This latter possibility may require increased expenditures for public relations aimed at obtaining local support. It is clear that centralization could decrease such tangible costs as yearly test development, competency identification, curriculum development, public relations aimed at the public at large, and test administration and scoring. However, such intangibles as state-local district polarization and teacher dissatisfaction may be aggravated by a high degree of state control.

The type of test one chooses has obvious implications for test development, administration, and validation costs. The choice of an available standardized test avoids development costs and may minimize administration costs, but increases validation costs. On the other hand, the use of a direct, performance-oriented, situation-specific measure may make the validation issue moot but be expensive in terms of administrative costs. A performance test may also be much easier to "sell" to test-skeptical publics than a multiple-choice test.

The number of competencies to be tested, and the number of items per competency, have a direct bearing on test development costs, especially for paper-and-pencil tests. The development costs of such tests are usually figured on a per item basis. Many of the school districts in Oregon, where each district administers its own program, began with lists of from 150 to 200 competencies, but reduced this to an average of 33 for reasons of cost and ease of test development.

The nature of the educational decisions that are based on competency testing has an across-the-board influence on costs affecting virtually every area of the program. In general, the more important the decisions to be made, the higher the cost. Several examples may serve to illustrate the point. First, when important decisions are to be made, such as whether individual pupils are to receive a high school diploma, test development costs would likely be much greater because the test will have to be technically above reproach. Longer tests would be required to increase reliability, and there would be increased likelihood, even certainty, that a contractor would be required for initial test development. Second, curriculum development, remediation, and legal costs would likely increase with the degree of importance of the decisions. Third, validation costs are directly related to the importance of decisions being made. School personnel, the public, and the courts will want to be convinced a test was valid for the specific situation and purpose for which it was used.

The failure rate one is willing to accept directly influences remediation costs. Quite simply, remediation costs increase with the failure rate. Additionally, high failure rates, especially beyond some unknown threshold point, would likely increase public dissatisfaction with the schools and would involve increased public relations costs in an attempt to offset such dissatisfaction.

The difficulty of the competencies one selects also influences costs. There is no doubt that some competencies are easier to acquire than others. To the extent difficult competencies are selected, instructional costs will increase. Anderson (1977) has suggested the probable relationship between difficulty of competencies, percentage of pupils expected to pass the competency test, and costs.

Finally, the frequency of testing influences costs in several ways. The most obvious of these is that there is a direct relationship between frequency of test administration and costs. Additionally, both initial and ongoing development costs may increase significantly with increased frequency of testing. For frequent testing, large item pools and parallel forms would likely have to be developed.

The discussion above is by no means intended to be an exhaustive one on the variables affecting costs. It is meant rather to indicate the complexity of the cost issue and the fact that the costs are highly variable.

Cost Estimates

Many, if not most, of the costs identified in this chapter are difficult, perhaps impossible, to estimate except within the context of a very specific program. Many of the intangible costs may not even be quantifiable. Program developers will have to anticipate the way in which different variables might affect cost in general and then weigh the cost considerations in light of their program goals and design. Disclaimers aside, a rough idea of ranges of costs can be made in general terms for several areas associated with a minimal competency testing program.

1. *Test development.* Costs run from $25 to $210 per item with an average cost of $100. Assume a test covering 30 competencies with five items per competency. In order to obtain 150 items after the pilot-testing, roughly 450 items are needed. Thus, one is talking in the neighborhood of $45,000 for test development. Since the tests might not be able to be used again, this could be a yearly cost.

2. *Test administration and scoring.* This is an area subject to wide variation. Figures range from 15 cents to $13.00 per pupil per administration. One factor which clearly affects this cost is the type of test one is using. For example, administering a commercially available standardized test would likely run about $3.00 per pupil. Administering, monitoring, scoring, and interpreting performance tests would cost even more. The authors' experience with administering and scoring writing samples indicates that the cost for each paper rated on only one criterion (i.e., a general overall rating of the paper's quality) would be around $6.00. If a greater number of ratings were desired, this cost would increase but not dramatically. For example, 15 criteria (i.e., separate components of writing) could be rated at a cost of about $7.50 per student.

3. *Remediation.* Select a percentage one expects to fail, and determine

the time to be spent on remediation, class size in remedial programs, and teacher salary to create a cost estimate. For example, if each child needing remediation attends three classes per week; a teacher teaches 21 classes per week; 210 students need remediation; and the average class size is ten students; then three teachers can cover all the classes. The cost would thus be three teachers' salaries plus all the ancillary costs associated with these salaries (e.g., fringe benefits) and a remedial program (e.g., materials, overhead).

4. *Bureaucratic costs.* Anderson (1977) reports state bureaucratic costs ranging from $65,000 to $945,000 per year. Local control may multiply these costs.

5. *Curriculum development.* Determine the number of teachers required to revise curriculum, the time required, and average yearly salary. For example, in one district, four English teachers worked for three weeks during the summer, average annual salary $12,000; cost, approximately $4,000.

The costs are many, possible variation almost limitless, estimates difficult to come by; but the cost issue itself may be of overriding importance in determining the nature and viability of minimal competency testing programs.

Reference

Anderson, B.C. The costs of legislated minimal competency requirements. Paper distributed at a series of regional workshops, September/October, 1977 on subject of minimal competency testing. Sponsored by NIE and ECS. Prepared with the assistance of a contract from the NIE.

Section III: Comparison of Two Implementation Models

The previous section overviewed a number of issues and concerns that may arise in the conceptualization or implementation of any minimal competency program. Thus, for example, concerns about purpose, need, and language are important regardless of the specific features of any proposed program. Similarly, the potential problems associated with teaching, testing, remediation, and setting standards face the implementers of all minimal competency programs. Finally, given the present climate, cost and legal factors must be attended to by the program planners. The issues discussed in the previous section, therefore, cut across varied programs.

However, some of these issues assume increased importance according to the specific plan or procedures adopted in any given minimal competency program. Thus, for example, the issue of state control of the curriculum—always an important concern in thinking about minimal competency programs—may warrant greater concern when a program is conceived and carried out by state agencies than when it is under local district control. On the other hand, costs for the program likely will be greater if each district must carry out its own program rather than capitalizing upon potential economies of scale available through a centralized state conducted program. Moreover, when the minimal competency program is tied directly to graduation certification, many of the issues noted take on a heightened importance.

In this section, we will describe two models under which minimal competency testing programs are implemented most frequently: a state controlled and administered program and a local school district controlled and administered program. Within each program model, we shall describe the potential problems and consequences most likely to arise when that model is adopted. Note that we describe *potential* problems and consequences, since very few fully implemented minimal competency programs at either the state or local district level are in operation.

The following chapter considers these two models in turn, providing a description of the model, implementation concerns, and needed resources. The critical policy issues which might arise if each model were implemented are discussed. In particular, the models will be discussed and compared in terms of such issues as: concern over local control of education, impact on the curriculum, remediation, establishing standards, measurement issues, legal issues, and costs. Obviously, it is impossible to elaborate all potential scenarios which might arise in each of the models presented. Instead, we endeavor to highlight many of the administrative concerns under each model and to describe the most likely consequences resulting from each model's adoption. As the following chapter indicates, there are benefits, liabilities, and trade-offs associated with the selection of an implementation model for minimal competency testing programs.

Chapter Eleven

Policy Implications of Two Minimal Competency Testing Implementation Models

Peter W. Airasian
George F. Madaus
Joseph J. Pedulla

There are many models under which minimal competency testing programs may be implemented. A sense of the variety of available models can be obtained by considering the three central aspects of a minimal competency testing program—(1) specifying competencies, (2) selecting testing procedures, and (3) defining standards of competency—and crossing each of these aspects with an agency or administrative arrangement which might carry out that function, e.g., the state, the local district, a regional center, an independent minimal competency testing authority, etc. Thus, a model in which the state defines competencies, selects tests, and sets standards might be implemented. Alternatively, local districts could be responsible for implementing the three activities. Responsibility for carrying out the activities could be split in many ways, e.g., state mandated competencies and locally selected tests and standards; state competencies and tests but local standards, etc. The possibilities are virtually endless.

However, of the many possible implementation models available, two have predominated. These models are state administration and local district administration; in essence, the two poles on a state versus local control continuum. This chapter provides a comparison of the potential policy implications of these two models in terms of seven areas: (1) state versus local control, (2) impact on curriculum, (3) remediation, (4) standards, (5) measurement issues, (6) legal issues, and (7) costs. Each model is described and the policy concerns under the seven topic areas discussed. We shall start with consideration of a state administered minimal competency testing model.

Model 1: State responsibility for specifying minimal competencies, establishing testing procedures, and setting standards.

Under this model, a state or state-sanctioned agency assumes administrative responsibility for the minimal competency program, including specification of competencies, determination of testing procedures, and setting of the standard of performance which will indicate minimal competence. In essence, this model is the most centrally controlled of the many possible implementation models, insofar as options within the program are limited. That is, the program encompassed under Model 1 is a state-wide program in which all districts and pupils within districts are responsible for the same competencies, tested by the same procedures, and evaluated in terms of the same standard.

A central concern in this model is, of course, "what agency or agencies should assume responsibility for carrying out these activities?" There are three logical possibilities. First, an existing state agency, the Bureau of Research and Assessment, for example, might be charged with the responsibility for administering the program. Second, a newly created agency—a Minimal Competence Authority analogous to the many state Turnpike Authorities—might be given responsibility for the program. Third, the entire program might be contracted out to a private agency or testing firm. It is also conceivable, of course, that these different groups could each administer one or more of the different program components, although this arrangement would probably complicate administrative responsiveness and efficiency.

In deciding upon the agency which should administer the minimal competency program under Model 1, a number of concerns should be considered. First, as noted repeatedly in this book, the issues of minimal competency are complex, both from a value and a technical standpoint. It is essential, then, that whatever administrative arrangement is selected, access to the necessary expertise to carry out the program be provided. Although this recommendation sounds both obvious and simplistic, the current ferment in Florida over the results of a recent minimal competency testing try-out points up the need for technical expertise in conducting a program. Second, the administrative agency must be acceptable to various special interest groups around the state. In this sense, a newly created agency might have the advantage of political viability state-wide, whereas an existing state bureaucracy might be tainted simply because it is a state bureaucracy. It is not clear how an external, contracted agency would be perceived. The longer a bureaucracy or agency has been in existence, the less neutral are the publics' attitudes towards it likely to be. Unless the administrative agency starts off with a reasonable amount of political viability across the state, implementation and conformity to the rulings of the agency may be difficult to obtain.

Finally, cost and time factors are important in deciding upon what agency will administer the state-wide minimal competency program. These factors should be balanced against the two factors just discussed. Creation of a new agency to direct the program may be appealing in terms of the likelihood of eliciting broad-based cooperation, but setting up such an agency probably will be time-consuming and expensive, especially if that agency is charged with the responsibility of carrying out the more technical aspects of minimal competency testing. However, selecting an existing agency to administer the program may increase regulatory, legal, and enforcement costs, particularly if districts balk over the viability of that agency controlling the program. Note also that diverting an existing agency from one task to another, while appearing cost-effective, might not be in the long run. Some states have wiped out their state-wide assessment programs and diverted personnel to newly established minimal competency programs. While this strategy may be cost-efficient in the short-term, it means that five years from now those states will have lost the ability to examine the effect of minimal competency programs on curriculum areas not included in the minimal competency testing program. At any rate, it is fairly evident that under a state administered model, a substantial bureaucracy is required to handle the tasks of testing, test construction, record keeping, test administration, certification, monitoring, responding to complaints, etc. In selecting an agency to administer the minimal competency program, the three concerns of expertise, public acceptance, and cost must be carefully considered, both individually and as they interact.

In Model 1, a single set of state approved competencies exists. In order to obtain credibility and support for the program, it seems important that the definition of the desired competencies not be left solely to the discretion of the administrative agency, but rather be based upon wide-ranging input from various interests and groups in the community. Thus, the definition of the competencies—and the direct responsibility of the administrative agency in defining competencies—should be separated from test construction and standard setting. The latter two tasks may be carried out largely by the administrative agency, while the former should be done through more broad-based community participation; definition should be separate from control.

The single set of tests of minimal competency in the state administered model poses some additional problems. It will probably be difficult to maintain the security of a given set of tests once they have been administered. This likelihood will mean that new tests will have to be constructed frequently. Moreover, in a centralized state-wide program, especially one which relates performance to high school graduation, it will be important to standardize many facets of the test administration process. For example, testing probably should take place on the same day or days state-wide in order to avoid problems of the tests becoming available to some groups prior to their being tested. This requirement, in turn, implies the need for some kind of bureaucracy to insure uniform test administration conditions across school districts. Mechanisms for distributing, scoring, and returning the tests and test results will also be required.

The above issues reflect general concerns in implementing Model 1. We may now turn to a discussion of the likely potential impact of Model 1 in a number of areas. In essence, the question we seek to answer in each area is "If a state controlled program is adopted and implemented, what are its most likely effects in this area?"

State Versus Local Control

In any model in which there is a single, state approved and mandated set of competencies, testing procedures, and standards, tension between state and local control of education is likely to arise. There are a number of benefits which may be associated with a minimal competency testing program such as that envisioned under Model 1. First, competence would tend to have a fairly uniform meaning across the state. With all pupils held to the same competencies and standards, there would be less variation in what a high school diploma means than is currently the case, although it is important to recognize that a great amount of variation would still exist. For those who perceive a need to bring uniformity of meaning to the diploma, a state model would likely provide a major step in this direction. Note that this model sets equal expectations for students across the state, but that equal expectations do not imply equal opportunity, equal achievement, etc. Second, a state administered program may have greater credence in the eyes of the public than a series of district level programs with different competencies, testing procedures, and passing standards. The possibility of some districts being labeled "easy" locales in which to obtain a diploma or to be promoted, thereby lessening the political validity of the minimal competency program in general, is reduced if all pupils in all districts must demonstrate similar competencies on similar tests to similar levels of proficiency. In the public's eye, there may be something "fairer" and "more rigorous" in having all pupils held to the same standards than if the standards vary from district to district. Centralized, state control of the minimal competency program therefore presents certain advantages.

However, these advantages must be considered in light of some disadvantages. A state administered model is likely to take least account of existing district to district diversities. Not all school districts are alike, and differences between districts are likely to be ignored under Model 1. Districts have different needs, types of pupils, teachers, resources, problems, and priorities. What will be the impact on this diversity of a program which requires pupils across districts to adhere to identical competencies, test procedures, and standards? What will be the impact on those districts which have already begun to institute minimal competency programs in response to their own local needs?

Given that a state controlled program is tied to graduation for pupils, it seems reasonable to expect that the competencies stressed will assume major importance for school districts. While this may not necessarily be bad—pupils will at least be receiving instruction in the desired competencies—it is likely that arguments about a state curriculum and infringement on local control will ensue. And in one sense these arguments will be valid, since the state, through its control of the minimal competency program, potentially will exert a strong influence on the curriculum and instruction at the local district level. Note that this influence is not general, as in many present state programs, but will be directed to particular competencies within particular subject areas. Any state administered minimal competency program inevitably will raise concern over infringement on local control and the propagation of a state-wide curriculum.

Impact on Curriculum

The impact of Model 1 on local school curricula will depend, in part, upon the extent to which the state-wide competencies presently are emphasized in local curricula. Potentially, however, Model 1 could exert a strong influence on local school district curricula for three reasons. First, local districts will not be in control of the testing and certification of their pupils and, thus, may be prompted to make an anticipatory response to an externally imposed, unknown examination. Second, the impact of the examinations on students, coupled with the lack of district control, will likely lead to an increased emphasis on the stated minimal competencies in instruction. Finally, the attendant publicity which undoubtedly will be associated with the implementation of a state-wide minimal competency program will increase parental pressure on the school district for satisfactory pupil performance on the examinations. A district's most logical response to this uncertainty, lack of control, and parental pressure will be to insure that the state-wide competencies assume a central role in classroom instruction. A move to a state-wide basic skills curriculum, an increased stress on basics, a reduction of emphasis in other areas, and conformity across districts are very real possibilities in a context in which Model 1 is in operation. Moreover, if enough pupils are failed or denied a high school diploma in the early years of a minimal competency program, there will be increased pressures on local curricula to conform to the state approved competencies.

These pressures are likely to be particularly strong in content areas which are not presently emphasized, such as communication skills. Verbal and auditory communication are not now stressed explicitly in most school curricula. If certification for a high school diploma or grade promotion is dependent on demonstrated minimal competence in these areas, it is to be expected that programs and courses emphasizing these skills will be inserted into local school curricula. Given a fixed daily time period for education, some other areas of the curriculum are likely to be de-emphasized to permit instruction in communication skills.

Potentially, then, for the reasons cited above, Model 1 may have a large impact on local school curricula. The issue of the impact on curricula should be considered within the context of two factors. The first, alluded to above, is the desirability of local options and control in light of local needs, as opposed to the desirability of a state-wide basics skills curriculum which might result from implementation of Model 1. The second issue concerns the phase-in time necessary for localities to make the necessary changes in their curricula implied in the adoption of Model 1. The amount of time, energy, and resources available to revamp existing curricula in light of state-mandated competencies will vary across districts and should be considered, especially prior to tying minimal competency test performance to high school graduation.

Remediation

Regardless of the minimal competency program model adopted, it is clear that remedial activities should be provided for pupils who fail to demonstrate minimal competence. Within the context of Model 1, however, there are two basic issues associated with remedial services. The first issue is who will pay for such services, an issue to be considered in a succeeding section. The second issue is the level at which remediation should be administered and provided.

It seems unlikely that the state agency in charge of the minimal competency program would wish to take on the direct task of providing remedial services in each local district. Doing so would require a gigantic bureaucracy. What seems more likely is that the state will leave the problem of remediation up to teachers and specialists in the local district. While this is a wise and probably efficient strategy, two potential consequences of this approach must be considered.

First, given state-wide competencies and the likelihood that many districts will have to restructure their curricula to meet these competencies, it is to be expected that resources within districts will be reoriented and reallocated. Efforts to remediate skills, knowledge, etc., which are not currently emphasized at the district level, will require a redistribution of funds and personnel from current activities. The pressure for remediation of the state approved competencies can therefore impact on local district discretionary funds and, consequently, influence the nature and types of programs a district can continue to provide. Such a result is a consequence of a local district having to provide remedial services in areas it does not emphasize in its curricula, but which the state requires.

Second, even though the state administering agency will not be responsible directly for providing remedial services to pupils at the local level, it seems likely that the state agency will want to monitor the local districts to be sure that its desires and policies regarding remediation are being acceded to at the local level. The state will want to be certain that funds earmarked for remediation are spent on remediation, that remedial funds are not being concentrated on certain groups (for example, those with the greatest likelihood of passing the competency test if given remediation) to the exclusion of other groups (pupils with severe learning problems), etc. In Model 1, one consequence of remedial activities, even though these are carried out at the local level, will be the need for personnel and mechanisms for monitoring local districts' remedial procedures.

Standards
The existence of a single set of state-approved standards in the various basic skill areas leads to a number of consequences. First, the problem of inter-district reciprocity, which can occur when districts use different standards, is overcome. Second, the standards for grade promotion or the high school diploma will have a more consistent meaning across districts. Third, the credibility of the high school diploma and the minimal competency testing program itself will likely be enhanced by the use of a single state-wide set of competency standards. These consequences are fairly obvious.

Two additional, perhaps less obvious, consequences can ensue from the use of a single set of state-wide standards of performance. It seems more likely that there will be challenges to state-wide standards on the basis of their unfairness to different districts or the standards' inherent bias against certain groups. For example, is it "fair"—and if so with how long a phase-in period—to compare urban pupils to suburban pupils on the same standards? Do resource, pupil, and other differences between districts require different standards of performance or different phase-in periods? Will disproportionate failure rates for different racial or ethnic groups lead to challenges to the state approved standards? The possibility of such challenges is very real in the context of Model 1. This, of course, is not to indicate that such challenges will be sustained, simply that they will occur and may move discussion of minimal competency programs from the educational to the emotional, legal, or political arena.

Additionally, the availability of district-wide pass rates on the same set of standards will lead inevitably to inter-district comparisons of performance. Such comparisons will undoubtedly put many pressures on local school districts. Some of these pressures may be beneficial in light of the purposes of the minimal competency program. Others, however, may not be beneficial, particularly when teachers, administrators, or school committee members are singled out or indicted for the performance of their district relative to other districts.

Measurement Issues

The consequences of a state administered program in the area of measurement are principally in the following four domains: administration and scoring, test validity, diagnosis versus certification, and comparability across districts. Model 1 calls for the administration and scoring of state-wide minimal competency tests. Due to the importance of the tests, assuming performance on them is tied to promotion or high school graduation, it will be essential for the state agency in charge of the program to exercise considerable care in standardizing the test administration and scoring procedures across local districts. Test security must be maintained until testing time. Pupils across the state's local districts must be tested at the same time and under the same conditions to prevent knowledge of the test and test content from spilling over from tested to untested districts. Testing days similar to those used for administration of the College Board tests, with similar administrative control and standardization across sites, will be necessary, if only to insure fair comparisons across pupils and to reduce the likelihood of legal action associated with inequities in the minimal competency test administration. The necessity for such standardization of testing procedures across sites will require, at the least, some form of monitoring or policing agency. Note the difference involved in administering minimal competency tests with important consequences tied to pupils' performance on the one hand and administering a state-wide assessment device to a sample of pupils in a school on the other. The former situation requires much more stringent control over the testing procedures than the latter and mounting a state-wide minimal competency program will be more involved than carrying out a survey of pupil achievement with no individual pupil sanctions applied.

Earlier in this book, a variety of test validity concerns as they relate to minimal competency tests was overviewed. It is most likely that challenges to the minimal competency program will come either in the context of the application of a uniform state-wide standard for certifying competence or in the context of the validity of the tests used to assess competence. Obvious validity problems ensue from the use of indirect measurements ("pick the misspelled word") instead of more valid direct measurements ("spell the word 'competency' ") and from the use of closely timed testing situations for tasks which need not necessarily be timed so rigidly (e.g., fill out an income tax form in five minutes versus fill out an income tax form within two days). However, other validity issues will arise as a result of the use of a single, state-wide set of competency tests to assess what inevitably will be curricular diversity across districts. While many of the consequences associated with the lack of match between competency tests and district curricular emphasis may be overcome with adequate phase-in periods, it seems likely that in the context of state-wide tests and state-wide standards which impact directly on the individual pupil, the state or state agency in charge of the minimal competency program will have to engage in some monitoring or policing of local districts to insure that the content of the state-wide tests is reflected in local curricula and instruction. Of course, as noted above, one consequence of such policing and monitoring is the threat of moving toward a state-wide curriculum, at least in the areas tested.

In considering measurement issues and their consequences under Model 1, one consequence which will *not* arise should be noted. Many people presume that the same test which is used to certify pupils' minimal competence will also provide useful diagnostic information to guide remediation. Such is not likely to be the case. While performance on the minimal competency tests will be useful for identifying pupils in jeopardy, it is not to be expected that a general certification test will provide diagnostic information specific enough to guide remediation. Additional diagnosis will be needed over and above that general information provided by the state tests. It is most reasonable that this diagnosis take place at the district level.

A final consequence of measurement issues in Model 1 is similar to a point made in the preceding section on *Standards*. The availability of state-wide test performance will lead inevitably to inter-district comparisons of performance. Such comparisons, in turn, can engender a series of pressures on local districts resulting from or accompanied by political and educational misuse of the test data.

Legal Issues

Legal challenges to minimal competency testing programs will be triggered by arguments of injury, primarily to students who may be denied a high school diploma. While denying a diploma to a student may not in itself constitute legal injury, the concern in minimal competency programs will likely center on denial of a diploma on the basis of a given set of tests and a given certification standard. Questions of racial-ethnic fairness, validity, timing, and the like which will form the basis for litigation are less likely to be directed towards the right of a state to implement a minimal competency program than towards the specific features, tests, standards, and sanctions associated with the particular program implemented.

In one sense, then, many of the consequences we have discussed in previous sections could form a basis for legal action, in particular, racial-ethnic bias, test validity, the mesh between tests and instruction, failure to provide remediation, inadequacies of test administration, etc.

The central problem in Model 1 is that it is state-wide and, thus, will tend to overlook, overgeneralize, or fail to consider idiosyncracies in local districts, from which legal challenges are most likely to flow. It is for this reason that the need for monitoring agencies to insure local compliance has been stressed throughout this discussion.

Moreover, it is not clear who will bear the brunt of legal challenges—the state, which mandates the program and controls its features; the local district, which presumably has some control over instruction; or individual teachers, who may be faulted for ignoring particular competencies. It will be advisable to examine the experiences of other states, Florida and Oregon in particular, to determine the most likely sources of legal challenge and the bases of these challenges. Further, it will be wise to consider specific methods for overcoming the bases for legal challenge by insuring adequate publicity and phase-in periods, validating tests and standards prior to their application, and so on.

Costs

On initial inspection, Model 1 appears to provide a number of economies of scale which may make it an efficient, cost-effective implementation strategy to follow. In some respects, this is true. Economies of scale result from: the need to construct only one set of competency tests for use state-wide, the need to compare performance against a single standard, the likelihood of centralized scoring, and the need for a single, state-wide administrative agency. Moreover, at the state level, it may be that particular hardware or distribution mechanisms already exist, thereby removing the need for additional expenditures to purchase or establish these. If we compare our estimated cost of about $45,000 to build a single, state-wide competency test to the cost for each district to build its own test, some notion of the benefit of potential economies of scale is evident.

While potential economies of scale and the reallocation of existing resources may appear to be appealing aspects of Model 1, there likely will be some new or start-up costs associated with the implementation of a state-wide minimal competency program. Initial publicity, explanatory materials, and test validation costs will be required. Of course, the cost-efficient nature of conducting these activities at a state level instead of reproducing them in each local district is still a reality in Model 1.

There are, however, two additional costs associated with a state-wide minimal competency program which must be noted. For the most part, these represent "add on" costs. The need for these two types of expenditures flows directly from the nature of minimal competency programs and their distinctiveness from other state-wide testing programs. In minimal competency programs, the performance of each individual pupil is of major concern because decisions about learning and competence are made on a pupil-by-pupil basis. We may contrast this approach with, say, a state-wide assessment program in which decisions about individual pupils are not of interest and data are aggregated across pupil samples. The sanctions and individual pupil consequences, which are a part of minimal competency programs, but not other, group oriented state-wide testing programs, may lead to additional costs.

Under a state-mandated, state controlled program, it would seem that the local school districts would have the strongest claim for additional state aid to support local remedial and extraordinary instructional costs. Depending upon the level at which standards of minimal competency are set—and likely varying from district to district—remedial costs may be large. Remedial costs may be pushed higher because, under many minimal competency programs, tests are not administered until grade eight at the earliest. This may not be the most efficient time to initiate remediation and, to do so, may mean a transferral of existing elementary remedial teachers to the junior high or the "add on" of new junior high remedial services. Funding for earlier diagnosis and remediation, which might have as its goal the correction of pupils' learning weakness *prior to* grade eight and minimal competency testing, would likely be the local district's responsibility. It is difficult to imagine remedial costs not rising under a testing system which puts a premium on *individual* pupil performance.

Given the possible consequences of failure—non-receipt of a high school diploma or retention in grade—it is evident that a state-wide program, such as that envisioned under Model 1, will require extensive monitoring and policing functions. We have described the need for standardizing test procedures, the necessity of insuring that remedial services are provided at the district level, and the importance of being certain that districts are providing pupils an opportunity to learn the state-wide competencies. The administering agency under Model 1 should not leave these issues to chance, but should implement procedures for insuring district conformity. The need for "inspectors" or mechanisms for certifying district cooperation will be pressing. Note again—and without belaboring an already oft-made point—that the reasons such monitoring activities are necessary is because of the consequences associated with each pupil's test performance. Contrast the consequences of minimal competency testing with those of state-wide assessment on the individual pupil, and the need for monitoring activities should be clear.

Finally, many states, in their rush to embrace minimal competency programs, have dismantled their state-wide assessment bureaus and reallocated personnel to the minimal competency program. While such a procedure may be cost-effective in the short run, dismantling assessment bureaus can prove costly, when, five years from now, someone wishes to know the effect of minimal competency testing on wider curriculum areas not covered by the competency tests. With no state-wide assessment bureau, answering this important question will be difficult and expensive. Consequently, one should think through the benefits and liabilities of dismantling and reallocating existing agencies to a minimal competency program in an effort to be cost-effective.

Model 2: Local district responsibility for specifying minimal competencies, establishing testing procedures, and setting standards.

Let us first examine and contrast Model 1, state control and Model 2, local district control. In Model 2, local districts bear the responsibility for drawing up a list of competencies in each area to be assessed (e.g., math, communication, etc.), selecting or developing appropriate tests of these competencies, and defining acceptable standards of performance. In keeping with suggestions that a broad representation of groups and interests be involved in developing a minimal competency testing program, especially in setting the competencies, Model 2 affords an opportunity to involve local people, close to local needs, in framing the program. Each district (or possibly a group of districts) could establish committees composed of representatives from business and industry, as well as educators, parents, students, and citizens. Thus, in Model 2 local people would be actively involved in the development of the local program. This involvement of representatives of local interests should increase the acceptance of the minimal competency testing program at the local level. It should be noted, however, that Oregon's experience shows that local districts were overwhelmed by the process of setting competencies and eventually asked the state to undertake this task.

The lists of competencies, tests, and standards, that are derived by different districts under Model 2, may overlap considerably. This overlap may be viewed as a disadvantage insofar as it represents a massive duplication of effort throughout the state. A state administered model circumvents this drawback by centralizing the process of developing a minimal competency program. Because of this centralization, however, a sense of local ownership of the program may be lost; there may be resentment at the local level because the competencies to be taught, the tests to be used, and the standards of acceptable performance were mandated externally. However, as noted, the single set of state mandated competencies, tests, and standards provides external credibility to the minimal competency program as well as helping to standardize the meaning of a high school diploma, something that Model 2 may fail to do.

A second consideration related to the two models is that some local districts in states not already mandating a minimal competency program have begun to implement their own minimal competency testing programs. It may be difficult to tell these districts that their work was for naught, and that they now must adopt the state mandated program. If Model 1 were adopted, some special concessions may have to be made to accommodate those districts which have an existing program. There are problems with making any concessions, however, including the danger that the whole state-wide effort could be undermined. Such concessions may be viewed by districts who have not begun a minimal competency testing program as preferential treatment, and this attitude could result in ill-will towards the new state-wide minimal competency testing program and even ill-will between districts. The trade-offs have to be carefully weighed under Model 1, if districts with existing minimal competency programs are to be dealt with differently from the majority of districts that do not as yet have such programs.

As said earlier, Models 1 and 2 may be viewed as poles on a continuum. Some states have considered implementing a form of Model 2, with each district's model being subject to state approval. The extent to which the state has narrow criteria of acceptance over locally submitted models is the extent to which the local districts really only have the appearance of control over their own minimal competency testing programs. In effect, actual state control over the three components of the model could be preferable to very rigid, narrow acceptance criteria by the state of locally submitted plans.

We will now focus in turn on the seven issues on which the two models presented here may be compared: (1) state versus local control, (2) impact on curriculum, (3) remediation, (4) standards, (5) measurement issues, (6) legal issues, and (7) costs.

State Versus Local Control

Obviously, Model 2 affords the maximum in local control over the minimal competency testing program. An issue under Model 2, however, is the credibility of the model. It may be that locally developed competencies, tests, or standards will be viewed skeptically by the public, whereas a state-run program may be seen to possess greater credibility. Again, there are trade-offs that need to be weighed between the issue of program credibility and the issue of giving local districts more say in the structure of their program. Another concern under Model 2 is whether the local districts have or will have the expertise and resources needed to mount such a program. Particularly for smaller districts, adoption of Model 2 may impose financial hardship.

Impact on Curriculum

Local districts may set their own competencies so that they reflect the existing curriculum. To the extent that this occurs, little impact on curriculum will result. State set competencies may have more impact on curriculum, but again this depends on how different the competencies are from what is currently in the curriculum. The nature of the competencies also relates to the impact on curriculum. For example, competencies in listening and speaking may result in greater curriculum change than competencies in math, reading, and writing, since the former are not currently emphasized in most curricula as heavily as the latter.

Remediation

Under both of the models discussed in this section, there is a need for a remedial component as part of the minimal competency testing program. With local districts developing their own program, there may be greater opportunity to obtain diagnostic information on their students and, thus, enhance remediation efforts. For example, a local district involved in developing its own minimal competency tests may find that much of its effort can also be applied to developing diagnostic tests to be given in the early grades. As a result, there may be greater cohesiveness or integration between diagnosis/remediation and the competencies required by the minimal competency tests. If local districts have access to staff skilled in test development in implementing their minimal competency testing program, this staff may also be able to develop a whole series of instruments which provide diagnostic information to teachers. In many cases, teachers will be able to provide pertinent diagnostic information based on their classroom experiences with pupils. Educational benefits to the students and teachers, other than maximizing the students' chances of passing the minimal competency tests, would accrue. In smaller districts, where it may not be feasible to have one or more people assigned solely to developing a minimal competency program, consultants could be hired or collaboratives of four or five districts could share a person skilled in test development.

Standards

As noted earlier, the problems associated with establishing standards or cut-off scores are many and complex. Not only statistical issues, but also political and economic ones impinge on setting standards. Again, someone with expertise in this area would have to be available to the local districts, if they are expected to set defensible standards for their own minimal competency tests.

More importantly, perhaps, is the issue of comparability of standards across districts. There would be no way to judge whether standards were uniform from district to district just from examining a test and the proposed cut-off score. The only way to insure that standards are uniform across districts is by empirical examination. Some students in District A would take District B's tests in addition to their own district's tests and vice versa. Comparisons between the two districts' standards could then be made on the basis of how similarly the two tests categorize the students. Of course, this procedure becomes muddied if the competencies for the two districts are different, since District B's tests may not be appropriate for District A's students and vice versa.

Further, although comparisons between districts may not be justifiable because of different competencies, tests, composition of the communities, etc., such comparisons will probably occur. Issues such as "District A requires only 70 percent correct for passing their tests while District B requires 80 percent" are sure to arise with the unwarranted conclusion being that District A is "easier" or less rigorous than District B. Problems may result from different districts having what appear to be, on the surface at least, different standards.

Finally, the issue of reciprocity between districts is particularly acute under Model 2. A student who transfers from one district to another, for example, may be tested on competencies very different from the ones he or she was taught. Concessions may have to be made under this model for students falling into this category.

Measurement Issues

Local districts could either develop their own measuring instruments or contract out this task. In either case, an added economic burden would be placed on the local school budget, but more will be said about this point in the succeeding section on costs. The development of instruments includes a validation process. Depending on how secure the tests are kept, test development (including validation) is an ongoing process. It is unclear to us if this validation process would have to take exactly the same form for Model 2 as it would for a state-wide test under Model 1. It may be easier for a local district to demonstrate that its tests accurately reflect its curricular emphases than it would be for the state to demonstrate that its tests accurately reflect the curricular emphases in all local districts. Evidence that the tests adequately measured what they were intended to measure would have to be obtained, but again it is unclear if this evidence would have to be as strong here as it would for a state-wide test.

Issues such as differential failure rates in urban as opposed to suburban districts may be partially circumvented when each district has its own program. The question would arise, however, as to the comparability of different instruments across districts. It may be that some districts will get a reputation for being "easy" and others "hard." A possible implication of this outcome may be migration to the "easy" districts by families whose children may be denied a diploma in a "hard" district. The task of assuring comparability across various districts' tests is very difficult. Empirical studies may help in the equating process, but the issue of comparability of tests across districts is deserving of very close attention in Model 2.

Another aspect of comparability between districts is the timing of test administration. Will all districts have to test their students beginning at the same grade, or can one district certify students beginning at grade eight and others beginning at grade ten? Will administration dates have to be the same across all districts in the state, or can some districts test on October 15, others on January 15, and still others on May 30? If each district controls its own program, state-wide standardization of testing time and procedures, as in Model 1, would probably not be necessary.

Legal Issues

The legal challenges that may arise are intertwined with many of the prior issues discussed. Local districts may be challenged by an individual student who is denied a diploma or by a class of people who question the whole testing program. It would seem that the potential for legal challenges may be lessened when each local district has its own program. This may be an instance where economy of scale works in reverse. Local districts currently make decisions that affect individual students, and very few of these decisions are subjected to legal challenge. This is not to imply that legal challenges will not occur under Model 2 but simply that the frequency of their occurrence may be less than under a centralized, state-run program.

If legal challenges do arise under Model 2, what form could they take? Locally developed instruments may be technically weak. Thus, a local program may be challenged on the basis of the technical, psychometric aspects of the tests. Some have questioned whether this is a real possibility, since local testing is already an integral part of local education; teacher-made tests are not generally technically sound, yet such tests are not generally challenged. There may be some weight to this argument, but when a single test, with the power to deny a high school diploma, is used, the situation may be perceived and reacted to quite differently than the teacher-made test situation.

Other challenges may arise from differential failure rates by various socioeconomic, ethnic, or racial groups. This type of challenge is more apt to arise in districts where there is a mix of these groups than in districts with more homogeneous pupil populations.

As a hedge against legal challenge, local districts may need to keep accurate records on each student, specifying when a particular competency was taught and attained or remediated. Local districts may also have to monitor staff to insure that each teacher is teaching the competencies and keeping accurate records on each of his or her student's progress toward attaining these competencies. Again, it is difficult to anticipate all possible grounds for legal challenges and the extent to which legal challenges will occur under Model 2, but the potential for such challenges certainly exists.

Costs

It would appear that the more responsibility each local district has for developing its own program, the greater its monetary costs will be. Most local districts are not currently staffed with people capable of developing instrumentation, carrying out validity studies, etc. Yet, people with this expertise are necessary if a strong and defensible minimal competency program is desired. Consultants or contractors could be brought in to manage the program, but cost is still a factor here. One could argue that the additional cost for a minimal competency testing program is well-spent, since it provides some evidence as to whether the remainder of the educational budget, certainly the preponderance of the money spent on education, is at least producing students who have minimal competencies. Testing and evaluation are often viewed as frills and expendable, when, in fact, they can be important components in justifying or in deciding how best to allocate the rest of the budget.

Nevertheless, the overall costs incurred under Model 2 will likely be higher than under Model 1. If there is no local support for Model 1, however, money spent on it may be money totally wasted, since the program may never become operational. In this case, the additional monetary costs incurred under Model 2 are certainly justifiable.

As with any model, development costs, legal costs, record-keeping costs, remediation costs, additional staffing costs, etc., must be absorbed under Model 2; the local districts may be hard pressed to obtain state monies for absorbing these costs, since the programs may be viewed as local programs. If the state is running the program or has a great deal of control over the program, as in Model 1, local districts may fare better in terms of the state bearing the bulk of the costs for the program than they would under Model 2. We are not merely talking here about state funds for the program *per se.* The related expenses that may be incurred from a minimal competency program, such as increased record keeping and remedial services, may have a better chance of being state supported or reimbursed, if the state has a more active role than it has under Model 2. This is not to say that no state funds would be available for this model, but that the chances for a greater amount of state funding seem better under Model 1. At the very least, local districts would have a better case for requesting or demanding state funds when the state controls the program.

Conclusion

At this point, the authors had intended to summarize the preceding comparison of models by providing a table in which the models were rated relative to each other in terms of whether they led to: (1) strong state control; (2) large impact on curriculum; (3) increased need for remediation services; (4) difficulty in setting standards; (5) many measurement problems; (6) many legal challenges; and (7) high costs. A table was laid out and a rating scheme devised. The authors then independently attempted to rate the likely consequences of each implementation model in terms of the seven areas.

The exercise was profitable—though frustrating—in many respects. Although we found that we could agree on a few comparisons, for the most part, we could not agree. Our lack of agreement, we realized, was a consequence of a theme that has been repeated many times throughout this book: the issues in minimal competency testing programs are complex and interactive, such that the consequences of any implementation model are dependent ultimately upon the contextual parameters into which they are introduced. In essence, during the process of trying to compare the two models on the seven criteria, each of us was imagining a different scenario involving different contextual parameters. Thus, under one set of conditions, a state administered model might lead to great difficulty in establishing performance standards, while under a different set of conditions the difficulty might not be great. Similarly, for either the state administered or the local district administered model, cost estimates are dependent upon a large number of other concerns, including, though not limited to, many of the seven criteria we were endeavoring to use as bases for comparison.

Our attempt at building a table that compared the two models dramatized the complexity of forecasting policy implications and the futility in attempting to provide a simple, one-dimensional summary of issues. Throughout this chapter, we have described the policy implications of the two models by means of a series of "if . . . then" premises; if such and such conditions apply, then this is a likely consequence, but if different conditions apply, then the consequences will be different. In retrospect, given the variety of contextual variables that may apply even within the implementation of a single model, this approach seems most reasonable. While it does not provide the closure that many readers will desire, it does serve to point out the complexity and interactive nature of implementation decisions, as well as their context-dependent nature.

Section IV: Overview and Recommendations

In this section, the editors endeavor to summarize briefly the major points and issues presented in prior sections and to provide recommendations for the implementation of minimal competency testing programs. As the following selection notes, the benefits of minimal competency testing programs may be great, so long as the conceptual and practical complexities of such programs are not overlooked in the press to implement programs.

Chapter Twelve

Overview and Recommendations

Peter W. Airasian
George F. Madaus
Joseph J. Pedulla

Although different in form and intent from other educational movements which have swept through American schools in the past 20 years, the minimal competency testing movement does share some similarities with its predecessors. Like many recent educational movements, minimal competency testing has achieved wide attention and adoption in a very short period of time; it has grown in five years to be a force to contend with in every state of the union. Also, like its precursors, it has served to raise the public's expectation regarding the success that schools will have in attaining desired outcomes. Earlier, people perceived compensatory education, open education, schools without walls, and similar approaches, each in its turn, to be the panacea which would cure the perceived ills of America's schools. Today, many see minimal competency testing in the same light. However, as before, these raised expectations are based much more upon hopes and rhetoric than upon clear evidence that minimal competency programs can produce desired ends.

The rush of activity in the area of minimal competency testing, whether based upon the expectations noted above or upon the sheer bandwagon effect of states and districts striving to "keep up with the Joneses," has produced another symptom which has been endemic to educational innovations of recent memory. That symptom is the tendency to overgeneralize and oversimplify, and it is based upon the failure to think through carefully implications, limitations, and potential pitfalls of new approaches. Attention has focused largely upon the end results that minimal competency testing is presumed to bring about, rather than upon the availability and suitability of the means necessary to achieve these end results.

A theme echoed throughout this book is that minimal competency programs, of whatever form, are not simple, but rather, quite complex. Implicit in any minimal competency approach are questions whose answers may have far-reaching and diverse implications for schools, teachers, and pupils. To ignore these questions or to give them short shrift in an effort to implement a program quickly can create untold consequences and attacks upon the program. Moreover, the technical issues associated with testing and standard setting, in particular, are neither simple nor unanimously agreed upon. There is a great deal of debate over the nature of tests suitable for use in competency programs, the types of validity and reliability these tests should possess, and the manner in which test performance should be related to standards which will be used to classify some pupils as "competent" and others as not.

In this book, we have presented papers which address many of the facts, issues, and uncertainties associated with the minimal competency testing movement. We saw that, for a variety of reasons, the general mood of the American public is one of dissatisfaction with the quality of education provided in schools; the public believes that too many pupils graduate from high school lacking the ability to read, write, or compute at an adequate level. We saw that, from both a social and technical perspective, the logical response to this perceived inadequacy is a movement which seeks to define essential skills to be required, test students to determine their level of competence on these skills, and certify pupils as "competent" or "not competent" based upon their test performance. The purposes of adopting this approach vary widely from state to state and from district to district. In some locales, minimal competency testing is intended to guide early diagnosis and remediation of pupils' learning difficulties. In other locales, the intent is to insure that grade-to-grade promotion is based upon pupils' demonstrated achievement. In still other locales, minimal competency testing is a primary criterion for awarding or denying pupils a high school diploma. These varying intents are wedded under the general banner of minimal competency testing by virtue of the fact that in all cases, pupils are tested to determine their attainment of a set of prespecified competencies and that attainment is compared to some standard in order to categorize each student as having demonstrated satisfactory or unsatisfactory learning. Hence, while different consequences may ensue from the student categorization (e.g., remediation, lack of promotion, or denial of a high school diploma), the general process of arriving at a categorization is essentially similar across programs.

Although apparently simple and straightforward in theory, the application of the minimal competency testing approach can generate many problems. For example, prior to implementing a minimal competency testing program, a series of questions should be answered. The first of these concerns the program's purpose. Is the intent to monitor pupil progress in skill areas at key grade levels? Is it to introduce a new basis for awarding the high school diploma? Is it to plan remedial programs? The answers to these questions to a large extent dictate the answers to succeeding questions.

The second issue which must be addressed before implementing a program is the nature of the competencies to be required. In this matter, wide choice is available. One can decide to focus on basic skills in reading, writing, and math. One may wish to emphasize the application of these skills in "real-life" situations. Other life-skills areas, such as citizenship, health, and various affective domains, may be selected. Associated with the selection of competencies is the question of whether schools can and should teach those competencies. Once competencies are selected and made public, the expectation will be that schools will teach these competencies to pupils. However, with dismaying frequency, one sees instances in which states and districts have failed to make a distinction between the ability to *state* a desired competency and the ability to *foster* that competency in pupils. We have suggested that schools can succeed in teaching most pupils to read, write, and compute. As schools depart from these basic skill areas and move into applications of these skills or into non-cognitive areas, their successes are likely to be fewer, simply because less is known about useful instructional strategies in these areas. We recommend, therefore, that careful consideration be given to the nature of the competencies selected, especially as they relate to present knowledge about instruction, and that initially at least, competencies be restricted to basic skill areas of the curriculum. Unless reasonably attainable competencies are selected, a program will run the risk of inflating public expectations about school outcomes with serious questions as to whether those expectations can be realized. In the end, programs with grandiose but essentially unattainable competencies run the further risk of exacerbating public dissatisfaction with schools.

Finally, at the earliest stages of program planning, it will be necessary to answer the question, "Who is to be held accountable for student learning?" In the 1960's and into the early 1970's, the failure of students to learn was laid largely at the feet of the schools. Schools were perceived to be culpable for failing to have the right type of experiences or motivators for students. The rash of federal programs in education in these years represented an effort to provide schools with the programs, resources, and facilities which people believed had prevented them from providing adequate education to all children. To a large degree, the minimal competency testing movement has altered this orientation. In most locales, whether consciously or by default, the onus for learning has shifted from the school and society to the individual pupil; it is the pupil who is accountable for his or her learning, and it is the pupil who is penalized for lack of learning.

We would not argue that pupils cannot or should not be held responsible for their learning. We do suggest, however, that the decision to hold pupils accountable be consciously and explicitly made. Many minimal competency programs, by default, end up holding pupils accountable, simply because it is difficult to hold any other individual or institution accountable. The question of who is to be responsible for student learning or lack of learning is critical in minimal competency programs and should be dealt with explicitly before installing such programs.

Once issues such as those just noted have been addressed, the conceptual groundwork will have been laid for a competency testing program geared to clearly defined expectations. At this point, a second set of issues associated with program implementation must be addressed. These implementation issues include technical and measurement concerns as well as educational, legal, and cost implications. The second and third sections of this book considered such topics in depth. While it is clear that not every issue within every topic which was identified in these sections will be of paramount concern in every minimal competency testing program implemented, it is also clear that implementation concerns are quite complex and extend far beyond the simple "test and certify" language used in many program descriptions.

For example, program implementers must decide whether they will use a norm-referenced or criterion-referenced testing approach. In the former, pupil performance takes on meaning when it is compared to the performance of other pupils who took the test; high or low, mastery or non-mastery performance is defined in terms of a pupil's standing relative to his or her peers. A criterion-referenced test compares pupil performance to the competencies of concern; performance is referenced to the desired competencies, not to the performance of other pupils. Each type of test has its advantages and disadvantages, each is constructed in a different manner, and each implies a different conceptualization of minimal competency. Moreover, regardless of whether one selects a norm- or a criterion-referenced test for use in a minimal competency testing program, a host of other generic issues arises.

Will competence be measured by paper-and-pencil techniques, actual performance situations, or some combination of the two? When will competency be measured: early in school, later in school, after schooling is completed? How will tests be scored to determine competence; will a total score be used or will a competency-by-competency approach be adopted? Can and should tests be kept secure, or should new tests be constructed annually? What types of validity and reliability are required for minimal competency tests?

As we have seen, the issues of test validity and reliability are particularly important in minimal competency testing and call for different strategies than those used in most other testing contexts. In minimal competency testing, decisions about individuals are paramount. Particularly when the consequences associated with failing a competency test are severe, such as denial of a high school diploma or retention in grade, it will be incumbent upon test users to examine the extent to which tested behaviors are represented in the curriculum and classroom instruction afforded pupils. From the standpoint of reliability, tests will have to show consistency of classification rather than many of the more common forms of reliability normally associated with educational tests.

Closely related to concerns over tests and testing are issues associated with setting a reasonable and defensible standard of performance to differentiate those to be certified competent from those not to be certified. Throughout this book, the complexities of standard setting have been noted. Standards have economic, political, and educational undertones. The measurement technology in education has advanced to the state where we can build tests—either norm- or criterion-referenced—quite well. Technology is less helpful when, given a pupil's test score, we must determine whether that level of performance is "good enough" to be certified as acceptable. How does one decide that 60, or 70, or 80, or some other percent correct is "good enough"? How does one determine whether he or she will fail 5, or 10, or 30 percent of the pupils who sit for a minimal competency test? Many different methods for setting standards are available, and references which summarized these methods were provided earlier in this book. However, as noted, all standards rely ultimately upon a value judgment and that value judgment is colored inevitably by the political, economic, educational, and personal consequences associated with different standards.

Standards *will* have to be set in order to carry out minimal competency testing programs. We recommend that implementers be aware of the inherent subjectivity in standards in making what is perhaps the most difficult decision in a minimal competency testing program. Further, we recommend that the viability of a given cut-off score or scores be examined empirically for a sample of students *prior to* establishing the score as the program performance standard. With such information in hand, the potential impact of the score in terms of number of students passing and failing can be considered.

The problems of selecting a testing strategy and establishing a defensible standard of performance are weighty and complex in their own right, but they are compounded by cost and legal concerns. A well-designed and implemented minimal competency testing program will not be inexpensive, so one cannot consider the nature of testing approaches or the consequences of different performance standards independently of the costs—both tangible and intangible, financial and human—which such decisions will entail. By the same token, temptations to cut corners in order to save money may increase the likelihood of legal challenges to the program, particularly when the consequences associated with failure on the test are grave for the individual pupil. Specific cost categories and legal issues which may arise in minimal competency testing programs were discussed in the second section of this book.

Finally, an additional set of concerns becomes relevant depending upon the administrative level at which a minimal competency testing program is implemented. In Section III, we saw that there are many potential administrative arrangements under which a competency testing program may be instituted. These models or arrangements were seen to lie along a continuum ranging from a completely state administered program at one extreme to a completely local district administered program at the other. Each model has its associated assets and liabilities. However, depending upon the model chosen, concern over issues such as state control of curriculum, reciprocity among districts, the meaningfulness of multiple standards of competence, costs, and recognition of inter-district diversities assumes greater or lesser importance.

In light of these issues, it is apparent that minimal competency testing is neither conceptually simple nor operationally straightforward. In seeking to draw together the many diverse threads which have been considered throughout this book, we provide the following set of recommendations or guidelines for those educators, parents, and concerned citizens confronted with the prospect of a minimal competency program in their state or school district. We recommend that:

(1) the minimal competency testing program's purpose be clearly specified at the outset, i.e., is the purpose to certify students for a high school diploma?, to hold schools accountable for teaching certain skills?, to decide on grade-to-grade promotion?, etc.;

(2) the desired competencies for the program be clearly specified so that all parties understand what areas are to be tested (it is *not* enough to use "catch" words, such as basic skills, life skills, etc., to define the types of competencies desired);

(3) careful consideration be given to the nature of the desired competencies, and initially that the competencies be restricted to the areas of reading, writing, and math;

(4) parties be aware of the fact that instituting a minimal competency program does not insure the desired results;

(5) legislation be carefully designed and worded so that schools can implement a legal program capable of yielding the desired outcomes;

(6) indirect pupil assessment measures be validated against direct measures;

(7) the program actually hold the desired parties, and only those parties, accountable;

(8) parties be aware of the fact that human judgment is integral to setting standards or cut-off scores;

(9) the implications of potential standards be determined through pilot-testing, prior to the program's implementation;

(10) a range of educationally, financially, and politically acceptable failure rates be established prior to the program's implementation;

(11) cost estimates—both financial and human—for the program be obtained; and

(12) the implications of the program, including the competencies selected, tests used, and standard of performance desired, on curriculum and instruction be thought through.

Further recommendations, not tied directly to the problems and issues overviewed here, are also warranted. States and districts newly embarking on a minimal competency testing program can learn a great deal from other states or districts who are further along in their implementation of a program. Unfortunately, answers to many of the questions which will arise are not readily obtainable in written form. Most often, persons in charge of ongoing programs must be contacted personally to obtain the desired information. We strongly recommend that such contacts be made. Lists of programs and their directors are available from the Education Commission of the States. To guide those states and districts newly embarking on a minimal competency program, we offer the following, more general recommendations:

(1) take a course of careful consideration and planning of the program even though this approach means more time before a program can be implemented;

(2) plan a strategy to insure that various publics, including politicians, parents, and school staff, are educated about what a minimal competency program really means in all its ramifications;

(3) alert various publics to the problems and implications of adopting a minimal competency program;

(4) obtain information regarding the minimal competencies that are common to, and those that are unique to, affected curricula so that appropriate lead time can be allowed for various curricula to reflect the desired competencies;

(5) form committees representing a broad cross-section of the community or state to finalize the desired competencies, thus lending credibility to the competencies and assuring support from the sectors represented;

(6) give careful consideration as to how special students, e.g., physically handicapped students, mentally retarded students, English as a second language students, etc., are to be treated under the program;

(7) validate tests to be used in the program with regard to how well they differentiate groups known, independently of the test under consideration, to have attained the competencies from groups known not to have attained the competencies; and

(8) do *not* tie performance on the minimal competency test to high school graduation, until there is evidence that the issues and problems raised in this book have been addressed satisfactorily; only then is it appropriate and valid to tie test performance to graduation.

The complexities of minimal competency testing are many and real. A number of states which have mandated competency testing programs aimed at tying pupil's performance to receipt of a high school diploma have delayed or are considering delaying the implementation of their programs in the face of the technical and conceptual issues identified in this book. The momentum of the competency testing movement has slowed somewhat in the past year, particularly as it applies to programs which tie demonstrated competence to receipt of a high school diploma. On other fronts, such as the use of competency tests for early diagnosis of learning problems or for grade-to-grade promotion, interest and activity remain at a high level. So long as the general public believes that schools are not satisfactorily teaching basic skills or are continuing to hold pupils to inadequate performance standards, the minimal competency testing movement will be with us in one form or another.

In spite of many dangers and uncertainties, the minimal competency movement does hold promise. After 20 years in which schools have been expected continually to expand their role in order to assume activities which heretofore had been the province of other social institutions, the cry is for retrenchment, for a focus on those activities schools have always been perceived to do best: teach reading, writing, and mathematics. To some extent, the lessons of the 1960's may have been learned: the school, in and of itself, divorced from other agencies and institutions, is not capable of remaking society or of inculcating pupils with all the skills, attitudes, and values they will need to get along in life. Schooling alone is not a panacea for solving all the political, economic, and cultural ills of American society. An implicit concern in the minimal competency testing movement is re-examination and redefinition of goals for schools and schooling. By re-examining, redefining, and narrowing the goals of schooling and by providing certification that students have attained these goals, the movement has the potential to restore public confidence in its educational institutions.

But more important, in many respects, are the issues which the competency testing movement raises for education in American society. Out of the competency movement comes a series of questions whose answers may provide an indication of where schools are going in future years. It is impossible to confront the spectre of minimal competency testing without addressing such questions as what schools should teach, what schools can teach, what are reasonable public expectations for the educational system, its teachers, and its pupils, and what is a "competent" pupil?

The minimal competency testing movement, for all its acknowledged dangers, is more than a new form of testing program. Potentially, it can provide the impetus to re-examine our educational system and our expectations for it. If questions such as the above are not posed, in ten or fifteen years the minimal competency testing movement will be little more than an historical curiosity, much the same as its numerous predecessors which emerged, created much fervor and activity, moved quickly across the educational landscape, and silently disappeared, leaving little in their wake but memories. If time is spent thinking through and confronting the many issues noted in this book, if we consciously strive to overcome gross simplification and generalization in the name of action, the minimal competency testing movement may do much of what it is capable of doing; increasing our understanding of schools, schooling, and the process of education. In accomplishing this end, the minimal competency testing movement may engender an educational system which is both desirous and capable of preparing students who are well-grounded in the basics of reading, writing, and mathematics.

Author Index

Subject Index